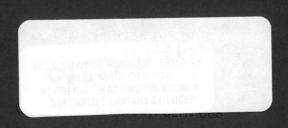

SOME BUSINESS OF AFFINITY

Some Business of Affinity

PAUL MERCHANT

FIVE SEASONS PRESS • 2006

Published September 2006 by
Five Seasons Press
41 Green Street
Hereford HR1 2QH, UK

www.fiveseasonspress.com
books@fiveseasonspress.com

Distributed in USA by SPD
1341 Seventh Street, Berkeley CA 94710-1409
www.spdbooks.org

ISBN 0 947960 39 2   *3757 1279 05/08*

Designed & typeset at Five Seasons Press
in Monotype Bembo Book 12.3/14.5 pt
(with Joanna italic for some single poems)

and printed on
Five Seasons recycled paper
(*paper specification / polemic: page 272*)

by Cromwell Press
Trowbridge, Wiltshire, UK

FRONT COVER:
Detail from stage two of
Dale Rawls's collage 'The Exiled Mandarin'
See page 60 for the complete image

*Five Seasons acknowledges
financial assistance from*

ARTS COUNCIL
ENGLAND

For the living and for the honoured dead who share these pages, and for one in particular who in four decades has shared a life.

ACKNOWLEDGEMENTS

Thanks to the following journals, where earlier versions of these poems first appeared: *Appalachian Journal*, *Granta* (Cambridge), *Gurukulam*, *Inca*, *Jefferson Monthly*, *Outposts*, *Planet*, and *Shenandoah*.

'Eight Views of an Exiled Mandarin', 'Bronze Door' and 'Barbarians Boxing' represented exchanges with Dale Rawls in *word&hand1* and *word&hand2* (Black Crow Publishing 2000 and 2002).

Pages from Coleridge's Notebook 21 are reproduced by kind permission of The British Library.

Poems and translations were broadcast by George MacBeth on BBC Radio 3 and appeared in the following collections: *91st Meridian* (ed. Christopher Merrill and Natasa Durovicova, University of Iowa, Winter 2006), *Another Republic* (ed. Charles Simic and Mark Strand, 1976), Berberis Press broadsides (2005), *Contemporary World Poets* (ed. Donald Junkins, 1976), *Green Horse* (ed. Meic Stephens and Peter Finch, 1978), *Guide to Modern World Literature* (ed. Martin Seymour-Smith, 1973), *Guinness International Poetry Competition 1972*, *Iron Bridge* (Other Branch Readings, 1983), *The Kilpeck Anthology* (Five Seasons Press, 1981), *Modern Poetry in Translation 4* (1968), *The Receiving End* (ed. Peter Medway, 1973), *Universities' Poetry 7* (ed. Peter Redgrove, 1965).

SOURCES

Catulli Carmina, ed. R. A. B. Mynors and editions of Catullus by C. J. Fordyce and Kenneth Quinn; texts and translations of Dafydd ap Gwilym by Idris and David Bell and by Rachel Bromwich; *Coleridge Notebook 21*, British Library MS Add. 47518 and Kathleen Coburn's edition of the notebooks; the collections of Cherokee materials at the Newberry Library in Chicago, the University of Tennessee Library in Knoxville, and the Museum of the Cherokee Indian in Cherokee, North Carolina; *The Diaries of John Dee*, ed. Edward Fenton, and Meric Casaubon's *A True and Faithful Relation of What Passed for Many Years Between Dr. John Dee and Some Spirits* (1659); original texts of Yannis Ritsos published by Kedros Publishers, Athens; Aeschylus *Persae*, ed. H. D. Broadhead; Horace, *Satires Epistles Ars Poetica*, ed. and tr. H. R. Fairclough, and Ross S. Kirkpatrick, *The Poetry of Friendship: Horace, Epistles I.*

Items quoted or referenced in 'Crossing Over with a Burden'— 5: Robert Herrick, 'Delight in Disorder''; 6: *The Return from Parnassus* (1601, pub. 1606); 7: Arnold Böcklin and Rachmaninov (*The Isle of the Dead*), and John Caleb Bingham (*Fur Traders Descending the Missouri*); 8: John Sibley, in *Discoveries Made in Exploring the Missouri, Red River and Washita* (1806); 11: Thomas Heywood, *The English Traveller* (1624, pub. 1633); 12: Elgar, Symphony No. 1; 16: E. M. Forster, *Anonymity* 1925); *The Greek Alexander Romance,* tr. Richard Stoneman (1991), and Ambrose, *De Moribus Brachmanorum*, ed. Ezra Pound (1956).

CONTENTS

ILLUSTRATIONS

The *Pinus sylvestris* motif (on the front board and blank rectos) is from a photograph by Julian Barnard. A pine-cone adorned the thyrsus carried by Dionysus/Bacchus and their Greek/ Roman votaries, pine was one of the three noble trees of Ancient China, and in Japan long-lived pines are celebrated as places of pilgrimage. In central Europe granite pine cones, about the size of a human torso, stood at intervals to mark the limit of Roman *imperium*, the edge of the uncontrollable.

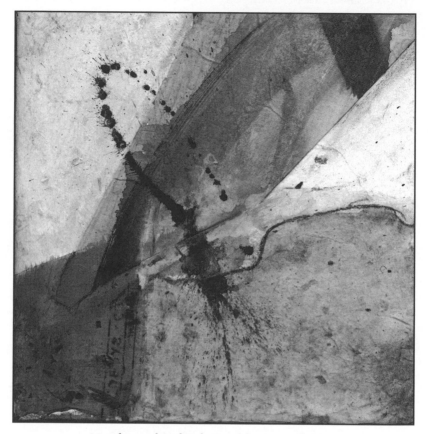

Number eight of Dale Rawls's nine exchanges
for the BRONZE DOOR sequence

BRONZE DOOR

From the Life of Catullus

An exchange with Dale Rawls

Sirmio

Olive trees, twisted, scarred, war-weary.
Beyond them the villa elegant among
cypresses. In the distance his lake, and
the Alps, its mother. A path curves
through the meadow, trace of daisies
in the grass. The world is ours so briefly.
Others made that path. Now only a scatter
of white flowers show where they walked.

Flute

Dawn is here, a blue light washed across
the window. He feels the god of sleep
unfold his dragon wings and flap away.
From deep in the house sounds the flute
of the girl from Colchis, a tune heavy
with longing, her hymn to the sunrise
over the Black Sea. When my father dies,
he says, this bird will have her freedom.

His Friend

He has been interrogating the little god
at the foot of his bed when he wakes,
who stands by him in the sleepless hours.
What do you offer, he asks, in return
for my devotion to the household gods
of kitchen and hearth? Nothing, the other
replies, the greatest gift of all. I am your
loneliness, the source of all your poems.

A Bowl of Olives

The bowl of olives sits untouched, as his
words fall steadily on the sheet, taking
their stations in the line. Behind him
papyrus rolls roost in their boxes. Each
made order from chaos, the little miracle.
It is late, almost dawn. He will ask the girl
from Colchis for a draught. She knows
potions to help him fall asleep for ever.

Last of the Name

A single cypress stands guard in the mist,
the rest of the world lost: his villa,
his grandfather's olive trees descended
from ancestors older than Troy. A ghost
has joined him. Memory of standing
at his brother's grave on that barren shore,
calling his name into the wind, Charon
in his iron boat long gone over Lethe.

Bronze Door

When did the last sun gild the garden wall?
That morning in Rome, carrying his words
of introduction, he entered a bronze door
into her courtyard garden, the murmur
of a fountain, flashes of silver carp
sporting in the pool. An undulating light
played on the lemon tree. Dazzled, he
turned. Her eyes were black as iron.

Storm

The reed-beds have felt it, swaying
away from the wind and the weight
of rain, the ripples shouldering through
the reeds, they let them pass. Lightning
sparks from a peak, and thunder answers
through the valleys. In the fierce scud
white-crests thud on the lake shore.
He wants to be a boat, out in this alone.

Another Sunset

All afternoon the horizon gathered clouds,
the sun dropped through them, leaving
bruises on their translucent skin. They
spread their battered arms across the water,
as if protecting it from something worse.
Daylight faded to black, another evening
closing its door. Night began its task
of storing up illusions, phantoms, dreams.

His Possessions

Before lighting the lamps he tallies
his treasures: the miniature landscape
by Zeuxis, that Sappho fragment, a shard
of drinking-cup from Socrates' prison.
What is it to possess anything? The curtain
(of patterned Persian gauze, her gift
when they were lovers) flutters across
the window, and he understands death.

Numbers

This poem he is writing will stand fifth
in his collection. How many more suns
before the long good night? Northwards,
the Great Bear, caller of souls, strides
over the Alps. A million stars. How many
thousand stolen kisses, sparrow-pecks?
Last year who would have counted
those stars, kisses, infinite suns?

The Last Muse

Yesterday in an uncanny light he saw
the muses one by one leaving the grove.
Mneme was first, carrying her box
of memories. Aoide followed, calling
a final line of song over her shoulder.
Last was Melete, his teacher from the start.
As her naked backside disappeared behind
a laurel he had a vision of Rome in ruins.

Owl House

Worn down by war, his grandfather shaved
his drooping moustache and was a Roman.
He perched this villa above the lake shore,
a mask with two windows, face of an owl.
It all outlasted him, the mosaic pavement
of abstract patterns, stone walls washed
with lime. The oak in the walled garden
burned on a pyre of crimson flame.

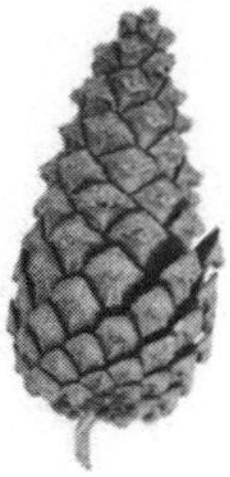

La Madonna delle Grazie between Zoagli and Chiavari
Dorothy Shakespear Pound

THE CONVERSATION ROOM

For three stranded travellers
who found the island with me

The speaker in these poems is Count Carlo Borromeo III (1586-1652), who began the transformation of Isola Bella on Lago Maggiore, close under the Alps. All of the names and some of the events described here are historical. Whether the count believed any of the ideas in these meditations is uncertain, but he must at least have been true to the Borromeo family motto 'Humilitas'.

Inheriting an Island

Later in the story
        a mountain moves
                but we begin with water

I dreamed of Babylon, a pearl earring
        a hanging garden in an oasis
                of rills and freshets

A world of rippled glass
        reflecting nothing, an island
                made indistinct by mist

Security is a castle with a moat
        or a vineyard on a south slope
                welcoming strangers

I inherited a rock
        surrounded by water
                a thin place

On the border between
        this world and
                our next moorage

Everything we regard is made of nothing
        the primed wall stands
                clean as a peeled egg

Then the first charcoal scratches. By day's end
        we see the ghost of a fresco
                that may be something

An Unsinkable Ship

The month of my father's death
        I rowed to the island
                least of my inheritance

And sat musing
        orphaned, desolate
                Arion on a stone dolphin

Across turbulence the Alps reared up. Back
        in the lee, farms and villas
                on rounded hills

Next dawn I brought my brother to possess
        our kingdom. Wind raked the lake to a cross-sea
                swamping the rowboat

Cesare the stronger
        pulled on the oars. I kept us afloat
                bailing with my crimson hat

On the island we laughed. The waves
        foamed at our feet. Our lives, a pageant
                of courts and palaces, never again so solid

Cesare died beyond our borders
        a meaningless skirmish
                on a chessboard of rice-paddies

I remember him, the day
        we half drowned, wind making
                a flag of his hair

'This rock,' he shouted, 'will be our
        argosy.' It was true: saved from shipwreck
                we built an unsinkable ship

The Art of Living

From the father come titles, servants
    a picture-gallery. Fidelity to our lord
        of Milan, and the arts of chivalry

The day he strapped a wooden sword
    to his belt, Cesare swung it
        like a fencing-master

On horseback he was a centaur. One
    June morning, he rode out through
        the gate of our courtyard

That quarrel over silk and rice
    like dice thrown from an unseen hand
        a musket volley met him as he vaulted a hedge

From the mother, secretly, the art
    of living. The crimson cap was her gift
        not to be worn in my father's sight

In the kitchen, alchemy of sweet
    and sour, salty and bitter. In the field Cesare
        dined on puddle-water and parboiled frogs

Canary Dance

And I learned the leaps and postures
      of that confection
            the canary dance

In courtship a unicorn and a peacock
      meet. As her father capered, I seized
            his daughter's hand

How nimble she was. I paced a stately
      round, fluttering my plumage
            with its hundred eyes

Le Gratie d'Amore. By day's end
      we had laughed and quarrelled
            and laughed again

Later she told my sister Isabella
      her namesake, 'That evening in August
            had the slow half-light of a dream'

Quarry

It was for her
      my new found wife
            we moved the mountain

Our summer villa half listens
      to the lake. Behind it a hill
            in its flank the wound of a quarry

Through this incision generations
      hauled pink granite. Blocks
            and slabs for the temples of Rome

Palazzi in Venice
      and our atrium
            glowed with the same stone

The plan, like all our enterprises, sprang
      from Cesare. 'Make that hill an escarpment
            and ferry its whole face here.'

So casually
      we commit ourselves to a task
            that becomes a life

A Pyramid

Cesare was our family's pharaoh.
     'To outlast ourselves,' he said
          'we build a pyramid.'

We recruited our private army, a regiment
     of boys. Most were grandfathers
          when the last stone was laid

To quarry granite, search out
     the softer veins
          and heat them with fire

Cold water, vinegar
     widen the crevices
          till a boulder is loosed.

At the hill's foot we waited
     with saws and chisels. A fleet
          of flat-bottomed sailboats

We prayed each morning to the gods
     of wind and water. Some days they woke
          from their slumbers and heard us

Time and the Moon

Time has swallowed up so many, a long
        retreating wave. We are left
               at the waterline, bleached, hollow

Her ink-black waterfall now a silver mane
        Isabella winds to a coil
               above that elegant neck

Haunting the spaces
        of this bare palazzo
               we are all but ghosts

Enshrined on their thrones, cardinals
        and saints look down. I am the doubter
               who plunged his fist in the wound

So as we age, faded beauty becomes lovable
        the moon when our shadow steals across it
               preserves her glimmering face behind the veil

Deep in My Chest

The past, of course, is never as we describe it
       but these are my memories now
             the others long gone into the dark

Evening has drawn in even as I was writing
       the candle roughens the sheet
             where my pen drags its shadow

Light scatters
       as if thrown from my fingertips
             into the room's corners

From the walls no answering gleam
       of gilded leather, no glint of oil-paint
             not even a saint's glory

I feel, deep in my chest, an iron hand
       tightening. Am I ready
             to meet that giant?

A Glass of Bardolino

This room is the palace's heart
      from here corridors stretch their arteries
         a current of life to every joint

Somewhere too far to hear
      my cooks are preparing a plain risotto
         of lake trout, with garden salads

I will raise a glass of Bardolino
      to the mother of our three sons
         bushes growing to trees

The youngster is the coming lawyer. The next
      who resembles me, will finish this building
         though without blistering his hands

His older brother, the ecclesiastic
      of the family, is already well suited
         for the cardinal's cap

I am certain to leave this work
      unfinished, like anything
         attempted in our sublunary life

Only a fool or a saint
      writes FINIS in rubricated letters
         at the foot of the page

To have poured my ambition
      into this shapely island
         gave my life shape

The Conversation Room

This chamber, the house, revolve about
    a circular table painted, you would think
        with a genre landscape

Flemish, perhaps? Look closer, see
    the filmy brush-strokes
        are tiny tesserae

Stone and glass, ranged like seeds
    of a sunflower head, ten
        thousand fragments of colour

Visitors from the world's corners
    each one a separate story
        if we could hear them

We call this almost empty
    space, this picture gallery
        the Conversation Room

Some talk that began here
    will echo after I am gone
        down the long corridor

Commedia

With marriage the scene fills. We have met
    the father-in-law
        and his almost silent wife.

Then the relatives, my brother the Capitano
    and sister Isabella the innamorata
        who married a constant prince

I am becoming, I fear, something
    of a Pantalone, stooped, myopic
        apt to brood on trifles

Our servants are witty
    and industrious, even in their roles
        as idle tricksters

In time every mask of Europe
    will pass across these floors
        share in our joys and losses

Revel at our feasts, applaud
    the musicians, laugh to see themselves
        mirrored on the stage

I too would laugh, but the commedia
    is deep, and at its discoveries
        sometimes I weep

The Lute

One day when the island held a world
        we said 'Tonight our arbors and terraces
            guard a thousand trysts'

I remember the King of Spain's visit
        two days to ferry his court from shore
            two years for our bank to recover

Our most welcome guest was a true Scapino
        a factor of the Muscovy Company
            sent to negotiate trade

We bargained furs, honey, and timber
        in return for olive oil and wine
            but our talk went everywhere

His wife, a quiet musician,
        borrowed from our music room
            a deep-voiced lute

And one night played the doleful cadences
        of the Englishman Dowland, visitor
            in a less fortunate time

I dared as we rose from table
        to exclaim to my friends, how filled
            with promise was our life

'Yes, that is so,' said my friend from Kiev
        his voice dark as a pine forest, 'but
            will we live to enjoy it?'

Under the House

The house has a secret
        not even the architect knows, who believes
            he can read my mind

Crivelli, who loves theatre, imagines
        our lives as pantomime, for which
            he has provided the stage

Above us the heavens, visited at night
        below, the underworld
            a haven for butlers and grooms

To reach the cellar, he built to my design
        a circular stair, supported on nothing
            but its own stone steps

This is the house's spinal column
        leading down
            to desire

There I have fashioned hidden grottoes
        the lake laps at the window sills
            the walls and ceilings shells

These caves are filled with shadowed light
        reflected from water
            source of all dreams

In one of the rooms a goddess
        sleeps on her marble bed
            any moment she will wake

Three Dances by Cesare Negri

1

Bound by love's chain
    he fashioned a melody linking
        lover to lover all the way back

As the dancers handed
    their partners to each other
        La Catena d'Amore

He wondered how many
    of those he had loved
        still lived and flourished

2

Peasants of a Piedmont village
    stomp their hobnailed boots
        in the *Nizzarda*

Then with what grace
    in the counter-measure
        they step and sway

3

At the edge of the cornfield
    the wind catches
        a crimson poppy

That bows and recovers
    then again inclines
        its elegant head

This dance between girl and boy
    Il Ballo del Fiore, repeats
        da capo al fine

The Play of Water in an Italian Garden

1
Running over pebbles
    the stream recites sonnets
        sotto voce in its own tongue

2
Water spurts from the stone lion's mouth
    where Isabella tilts her face
        under the torrent

3
Cascading laughter, poured wine's murmur
    jet of conversation
        cool touch of a lover

4
The dependable sun greets the trees
    where they lean over light translated
        into shadows and inconstancy

5
This pool
    remembers its days
        in the clouds

6
The bronze frog
    and the stone turtle
        startled, both jump together

7
The noon sun will roast every creature. Come
    under this cedar, enjoy the water
        cascading over naked Nereids

8

The fish
    in the lily pond
        think they are whales

9

Water sings to rock, 'Wait
    for me here, till I come
        to carry you away'

10

The fountains are lake water
    raised by an old horse
        treading his round in the pump house

11

Marble, she carries her urn into eternity, pouring
    its contents along her flank. Two
        nymphs bask in this instant of sun

12

From here
    the lawn
        is a green lake

13

White peacocks are spirits
    of the island. Their hoarse cry reminds us
        of a sun-scorched rock

14

Gold fish dance
    their galliards
        to the quavering music of flies

15

Bathing, he spills quicksilver
    down his back. In the whole garden
        the only darkness is the blackbird's coat

Paradiso

I have set an angel
      with a flaming sword
           to guard this garden

He is unshaven, a cherubim
      in disguise, and his sword a stick
           for his arthritic hip

We call him the grandfather
      he plays my part perfectly
           when I am travelling

If this palazzo and its garden
      were a body, Isabella
           would be its soul

How strange
      but she will outlive me
           alone at the long table

Soon after I am gone
      she will leave the island
           which is the world

And enter that most spacious of rooms
      a convent cell. Our son the cardinal
           will arrange everything

I approve her choice
      the last costume we put on
           should be simplest of all

Razullo. Cucurucu.

A Gift from Callot

It is all show. The zany with the long-necked
lute singing 'Lucia my darling' under
an imaginary window. A scarf hangs
on the peg of his erection. The second mask
pretends a strutting dance, all hand signals
and feathers. Any moment now the cockerel
may crow. He repeats, for want of a better,
his usual gag, 'How well she knows me.'

But wait. This is real. The Piedmont sun
touches the plump buttons on their doublets,
throws shadows on the cobblestones. Other
spectators crowd around a stage, a story,
a life they recognize. Here for an instant
we have speaking parts in this farce.

---

from Jacques Callot, *Balli di Sfessania*

LAZY DAY BLUES

A Selection from Catullus

Cᴠɪ DONO LEPIDVM NOVVM LIBELLVM

ARIDA MODO PVMICE EXPOLITVM?

CORNELI, TIBI: NAMQVE TV SOLEBAS

MEAS ESSE ALIQVID PVTARE NVGAS

IAM TVM CVM AVSVS ES VNVS ITALORVM

OMNE ÆVVM TRIBVS EXPLICARE CHARTIS

DOCTIS, IVPPITER, ET LABORIOSIS.

QVARE HABE TIBI QVICQVID HOC LIBELLI

QVALECVMQVE; QVOD, O PATRONA VIRGO,

PLVS VNO MANEAT PERENNE SÆCLO.

Catullus was a provincial from Verona, in Cisalpine Gaul, but seems to have been most happy in his villa by an Alpine lake, Benacus (now Lago di Garda). The two momentous events in his life were the meeting with 'Lesbia' (Clodia Metelli) and the death of his brother. Thrown in among the famous poems of adoration and hatred is an outpouring of witty squibs, translations from Greek, odes, obscene libels, and long meditations. Catullus died at the age of thirty, having already found a personal voice as vivid as Sappho's. He left to all the Romance languages the Celtic word for a kiss.

I

[1]
Who'll handle this fresh little book, this
smart, scrubbed, polished little book?

My friend, you liked these jottings, so
you said. And you put all of history
into three fat tomes. Good god, who else
in Rome would try a stunt like that?

It's your turn, make what you can
of this collection.
                    And Lady Muse,
keep it alive at least one generation.

[51]
He could be a god, or even
(god forgive me) something
greater, sitting close to you
            gazing and hearing

Your gentle laughter's gentle
death-blow. First sight of you
Lesbia, I was lost already
            lost without language

Stammering, my whole skin urgent
flame-like, ear-drums thudding
with blood, my eyes in darkness
            stranded and fog-bound.

(Later)
Time, time on your hands, Catullus,
time drifting through your fingers.
Time buried kings before you, and
            the wealth of their cities.

[5]

Lesbia, time to love and play.
Let the joyless old folks bray
their trivial complaints today.
Suns can set and re-ignite.
We blaze in temporary light
before we sleep an endless night.

Time for kisses, twenty, ten,
ten, then twenty, ten again.
Ten times twenty more, and then
scramble the abacus of our bliss.
We hardly need our every kiss
tallied by some sneaking miss.

[7]

How many kisses will it take
(Lesbia asks) my love to slake?
As many grains of Libyan sands,
where Zeus's sweltering oracle stands,
home of the love-charm silphium,
near ancient Battus' family tomb.

The stars that in the silent sky
observe our amatory plots,
that sum of kisses will requite
your crazed Catullus' appetite,
confound the calculating spy
and tie his jealous tongue in knots.

[2]
Sparrow, my girl's delight,
she teases you, you hop
on her lap, she holds out
a fingertip, you bite it hard.

With my bright lady-love you
play such games, they tame
her lust. Cool, I trust, the embers.

I'd play with her like that.
I'd lift her spirits, too.

[3]
You gods and goddesses of love, and
heartsick humans, time for tears:
my sweetheart's sparrow's dead,
that sparrow she delighted in,
apple of her pretty eyes.

Honey-sweet, her favourite,
he stayed so close (as a girl
clings to the apron-strings) he
hopped away only a step or two
chirping for her and only her.

Now he's on that unlit road
they say no traveller retraces.
Shame on you, gods of darkness,
who snatch the sweetest morsels,
for stealing away my sparrow.

Poor sparrow. Death, you villain,
you made my lady weep,
her pretty eyes are swollen.

[13]

Fabullus, come to dinner at my table
if fate decrees, in just a day or two.
And you'll eat well, Fabullus, if you're able
to bring the dinner and a girl with you.
Oh, wine as well, and wit, the latest joke,
bring these along with you, my dearest friend,
you'll eat your fill. It seems Catullus' poke
is spun with spider webs. Nothing to spend.

My part? I'll pour love straight from the flask,
and something smoother, richer even than love.
I'll share a scent. My girl's scent, since you ask,
her gift from all the goddesses above.
Fabullus, come inhale. Your prayer will go,
'I want to be all nose, from top to toe.'

[43]

Ameana, with your nose (not small),
your feet (not dainty), eyes (not dark),
fingers (not slender), lips (not dry),
voice (not quite melodious), you're
bankrupt Mamurra's choice.

And Gaul calls you a beauty,
compares you with Lesbia?
We live in barbarous times.

[17]
Festival frenzy, Verona, on your long bridge,
time to dance, except that the poor thing's
wobbly shanks, buttressed by salvaged planks,
would buckle, send it sprawling in the marsh.

Today it needs to meet your every wish
as a stage for the rites of Salisubsalus,
so I propose a not so serious solution:

There's a citizen I'd catapult off your bridge
head over heels in the mud, choosing
the deepest, greenest, bottomless abyss
where the lake water's at its smelliest.

The man has no more wit than an infant
asleep in the arms of his doddering dad.
He's married the freshest flower in the field,
a girl friskier than a baby goat, precious
as succulent black grapes. Handle with care.

He lets her play as she pleases. He's oblivious,
nothing at all to offer, prone like an alder
thrown in a ditch, hamstrung by a Celtic axe,
this log, unfeeling, stupid, dead to the world.

Idiot, he realizes nothing, listens to nobody.
Does he exist? To him that's a mystery too.

He's the one to send from the bridge. The fall
may jolt him out of his ancient lethargy,
leaving his spineless soul sprawled in the mire
as a foundering jackass loses his iron shoe.

II

[65]

This pain, Hortensius, masters me. It ends
my dialogue with the learned girls. Tossed about
in such wild sea-tempests, my heart is closed
to the Muses and their seductive gifts.

Even now that thief of memory, Lethe
laps at my brother's bloodless feet, where
he waits for passage. His body lies buried
in Trojan earth, spirited out of sight.

And the Muses are silent. No word
to tell if we will meet again, brother
dearer than life. Only love survives
in this poem I fashion for your death.
I am the nightingale in leaf shade
mourning her murdered child.

Out of that agony, Hortensius, I send
this new translation from Callimachus,
reminder that your words were heard,
not thrown to the ever-wandering winds
as an apple, secret gift from a lover,
leaps from a young girl's dress.

She left it in her lap and forgot it there.
Her mother comes, she starts, it tumbles loose,
bumps along the floor, rolling and rolling.
A guilty blush floods her tear-stained face.

[46]

Spring. Soft unfrozen air,
the sky's midwinter storms
gentled by calm-sea-breezes.

No more Troy, Catullus,
Bithynia's sweltering cornfields.
Asia's tempting cities call.

My mind is eager to wander,
my feet are restless too.

Dear friends, travel companions
journey safe to your distant homes
your several destinies.

[101]

I came from another world, crossed a wide sea
to stand at your barren scratch of a grave

Carrying my farewell gift to you, words
addressed to dust, a pointless monologue.

Chance stepped between us, my brother,
and snatched you out of my sight,

Now all I can offer are the appointed
tokens: wine, milk, honey, flowers,

And a brother's tears. No help for it.
I came here. We will never meet again.

[31]
Sirmio, prettiest of islands or
almost-islands ruled by Neptune
in sweet or salty guise,
light of heart, I drop anchor,
Bithynia's fields forgotten.
Am I truly home and safe?

Ah, to set cares aside! The mind
lays down its burdens. Tired
from toil at the world's edge
we reach our hearth, our bed.
After such labour, what joy.

Lovely Sirmio, greet your master.
And Etruscan water, let me hear
that familiar rippling laughter.

[4]

I'll take you after dinner to see my boat.
The quickest ship afloat, she claims.
No piece of timber launched on water
could outrun her, rowing or under
canvas. She can prove it. She's been
everywhere: the moody Adriatic,
stately Rhodes, the scatter of
smaller islands, bristling Thrace,
the Bosphorus and rough Black Sea,
where in her youth this future yacht
graced as a waving wood the ridge
behind Cytorus, whistling Asian tunes.

On the Black Sea, Amastris by Cytorus,
she had her childhood home, that's
my boat's story. Yes, there was a time
she topped their highest hill. Those were
the waters where she learned to swim,
where first she breasted breakers
to bring me safe through life's worst
tempests. She could tack as easily
as run with the wind, lively in all seas
fair or foul. Not once did she call out
for shore-gods' help to keep afloat
on our last journey to this crystal lake.

That's her history. Laid up at last she feels
age season her, under the sailor's sign,
the Dioscuri: Castor and Castor's twin.

III

[10]

Come see my new girlfriend, said Varus
in mid Forum, so I kept him company.
For a tart, I saw at first glance, she wasn't
without intelligence, and she was easy
on the eye, so we got to talking about
this and that, but mostly about Bithynia,
how well we all made out back there
and how many perks brought home.

No need to wrap up the truth, I said,
none of us, governor or staff, did well
out of it, mostly on account of the boss,
about whom the less said the better,
treating all his staff like dirt. But surely,
chimed in the others, at least you formed
a squad of litter-bearers, Bithynia
being the place for litter-bearers?

She was a good-looking girl, I couldn't
resist a small untruth. Pickings were slim,
I said, but I managed to find myself
eight upright men to carry me around.
The truth is, I couldn't hire a beggar
with either strength or inclination
to hoist a broken bed leg. But she,
the little vixen, piped up again:

Darling, dear Catullus, do me a favour,
let me borrow your men. I need a ride
to the festival of Serapis. Hold it
right there, I said, my memory's not
what it was, they're not mine, they're
Cinna's, my old pal Gaius Cinna. Oh
what the hell, mine or his, we share
and share alike. But as for you,

You tactless slut, isn't a man allowed
to make a mistake occasionally?

[53]
A wag in the peanut gallery made
a good joke, when my pal Calvus
was building his case against
Vatinius. He stretched, and said,
'Good God, this froggy can croak!'

[26]
Your cottage has a prospect, Furius.
To the sharp east wind or northern blast?
To hot siroccos, or to westerlies? No, you've
blown away a cool two million smackers.
I'd want some shelter from that draft.

[105]
The Sacred Mount. Mamurra tried to ascend it.
The Muses rushed with pitchforks to defend it.

[95]
Cinna's epic's here—nine summers
and nine winters in gestation.
Hortensius, meanwhile, in a single year
gave birth to fifty thousand mice.
Cinna's poem will cross the seas
to be read when history itself is old.
Volusius' annals will fail in Padua
ending their days as mackerel wraps.

[50]

Yesterday, Calvus, nothing to do, we
played lazy day blues on the keyboard,
two cool customers doing their thing
giving each other poem starts, a game
of pitch and toss with metrical schemes,
passing the bottle, having the last laugh.
I came away high as a kite, Calvus,
lit with your wit, your quick ripostes.
Now I'm off my feed, no appetite,
not a bite, no respite for weary eyes,
tossing and turning all over the cot,
white-hot, awaiting day's light, ready
to start all over the whole palaver.
Dawn. Worn to a shred, half dead,
spread supine on my little bed,
came to me, dear flame, this riff,
a whiff of my despair, a prayer.
Take care, light of my life, don't dare
ignore this love-note shipped to you.
Nemesis will whip you black and blue,
and she's a boss you'd best not cross.

[59]

Dateline Bologna: Rufa sucks her brother dry.
She's married to Menenius, but her supper
(you know) comes from the cemetery.
She grabs a loaf that's fallen from the pyre
as she's banged by the bristly undertaker.

[45]
Septimius, Acme in his lap
had this to say: 'Acme, my dear,
if I don't love you to perdition
down all the centuries
as much as man can love,
may I be dinner to a green-eyed
lion in Libya or toasty India.'
He was done. Over both his shoulders
the love-god sneezed approval.

Acme, tilting back her head
to kiss his love-besotted eyes
with rosy lips, replied:
'Seppy, love of my life,
let's be forever Cupid's slaves
as long as this keen fire
runs in my marrow-bones.'
She was done. Over both her shoulders
the love-god sneezed approval.

An excellent start, both parties launched
on a journey of change and exchange.
Septimius chooses Acme's kisses
over serving in distant Britain.
Devoted Acme offers Septimius
sole access to her charms.
Who ever saw a happier pair,
a more promising love?

IV

[70]
Lesbia (married) says I'm her man: 'No one,
not even the high king of heaven,' etc., etc.
Whatever she thinks you want to hear, words
on the wind, scribbled in running water.

[72]
Lesbia, you used to call Catullus
your only choice. You'd refuse a god.
My love for you? It was helpless,
a father's feeling for his only child.

My eyes are opened. White hot, I find
that old attachment stale and trivial.
A paradox? The wounded suitor feels
his lust persist as admiration fades.

[58]
Caelius, our Lesbia, yes, that Lesbia,
that Lesbia, Catullus' only love
(a love beyond self, beyond family)
on every corner, down every alleyway
fleeces the sons of noble Romulus.

[8]

Don't be a fool, Catullus. Stop right there.
What's lost is lost. A bad debt, written off.
There was a time the sun shone bright.
You'd trail behind, wherever that girl led.
Your only passion. Never again such love.
Those were the carefree years, all play.
What you desired, she had the same desires.
Those days indeed the sun shone bright.
Now she's grown cold. Turn cold yourself.
Don't follow when she runs. Don't mope.
Take courage. Chisel a heart from stone.
It's over, girl. Catullus' heart is stone.
No looking out for you, inviting you.
How sad you'll be. No invitations now.
You're ruined. What kind of life is left?
Who'll wait for you and praise your looks?
Who'll be your love? Who'll call you his?
Whose mouth will you kiss? Nibble his lips?
No choice, Catullus. Make your heart stone.

[85]

I loathe her. Still I love her. How can that be?
A mystery, I feel it happen. Agony.

[11]

Furius and Aurelius, old mess-mates,
try these brochures: 'Farthest India'
(sunset, the eastern ocean thudding
     on a long shoreline)

Or 'Overland with a Camel Caravan'
(run the gauntlet of warring tribes)
or 'Back to the Med' (its waters
     reddened by Nile floods)

North, perhaps? 'An Alpine Scramble
In the Footsteps of Caesar' (across
Germany to Britain, lost in the ocean
     right off the world's rim)

Any of these you said, with god's help,
you'd sample. Take then, if you dare,
this message (short but not sweet)
     meant for my darling:

Long life and health! Happy adulteries!
(all three hundred in a single clutch
like a vampire, loveless, methodical
     sucking them bone-dry)

I adored her. Forget that. She destroyed
my love. (It was a flower blossoming
in the field corner. A ploughshare
     touched it and went on.)

Dale Rawls: all three stages of
the *Exiled Mandarin* exchange

EIGHT VIEWS

OF AN EXILED MANDARIN

An exchange with Dale Rawls

Evening Snow

Lamplight falls from my window
square on the snow's blank screen.
In the shadows but not forgotten
ten thousand desires lie curled.
High in the tallest pine a bird
calls out a plaintive cadence.
My friend the cat looks up at me,
her face transfigured by greed.

Autumn Moon

The moon's boat sails alone tonight
through choppy clouds. And did it gleam
in your sky too, with its single star?
Remember the grove with its ancient
oak trees, their branches joined
across four hundred years? The world
is not too large. I feel you close,
an orange slice exploding in my mouth.

Clearing Weather

Mists have filled the whole valley,
even the road from my door is erased.
Beyond the mist, is there a mountain?
I saw it yesterday, white in sunlight
but that was yesterday. On the verge
of the shadowed road my ghosts
stand waiting, just out of sight.
Any small thread will draw them back.

Evening Bell

The enormous half-moon, pale, pockmarked, casts
its grey light on the lake. That smudged cloud
catches the last flicker of red, as a bell tolls
day's end across the quiet water. A heron
standing over his snaky reflection and a little owl
on his low branch watch for careless moments.
A duck and her last duckling are ready for sleep
on a floating log, beaks tucked under their wings.

Fishing Village at Sunset

Across an ocean thirty years wide the sun,
round and succulent as an orange, touched
the horizon, that still evening moment. Light
slanted across whitewashed houses, a stone jetty,
the mended nets spread out to dry, a bleached
crab shell among the pebbles. "When I die,"
that quiet voice beside me said, "I want to fade away
to nothing." Behind her the sea was black as ink.

Wild Geese in Last Light

As night mingled with dark water we could hear
the sea's long fury. Offshore, marooned in darkness,
the great rock endured its battering. Beyond it lay
cities so distant only their names were real. Suddenly
above us the shadow of a ghost ship appeared
on the purple sky, wild geese flying south at last,
a galley rowed by slaves from a conquered country
calling to each other in their harsh forgotten tongue.

Boats Returning at Evening

They heard through the open door the ocean
grinding its pebbles, and the fishermen's songs
out in the bay. The cook brought to the table
two mackerel on a black lacquer tray. It was
so long ago. He tried to place the shoreline,
the striped tablecloth, the shredded ginger,
but realized his memory had the misted
outlines of an event that was still to happen.

Night Rain on the River

From the teahouse on the far bank the plucked
notes reached their ears, raindrops dripping
from the eaves of an abandoned temple.
They listened to the music that was water
carried on water. It was joined by a flute
breathing its urgent message. They sang
till they were satisfied. Their thoughts fell
like rain on the river, and were swept away.

Hokusai: *Hotei*

In 1834 Katsushika Hokusai published the first
volumes of his masterpiece *One Hundred Views
of Mount Fuji*. He was seventy-three years old, at
the height of his powers, and impoverished. He
continued to paint with undiminished skill until
his death at the age of ninety.

THOUGHTS OF AN OLD MAN

CRAZY ABOUT PAINTING

Mist

When I could handle chopsticks, my parents
sold me to a rich man, a maker of mirrors
at the shogun's court. For years I polished
surfaces reflecting the ten thousand things.
On their backs I engraved erotic couplings.

We begin and end (let no-one tell you
otherwise) in mist. I remember sunlight
striking a steep ridge. Below me the river's
pewter gleam, four boats drifting, aimless.
The fish still deep in the chilled water.

There was an inlet, serving a tiny village
of thatched houses. An impenetrable mist
six decades deep rolls in. Was the mountain
there that day? I recall only the spring's
pale sun opening the scarlet maple buds.

They climbed past me on the hill's flank,
four men and a girl, with rakes and mattocks,
baskets slung for mushrooms. On her hip
she carried a pouch. Her thick hair bunched
into a mare's tail, the men hunched, balding.

I remember now her over-kimono scattered
with plum blossoms tucked up at her waist,
the dark blue sash. She strode up the slope
and was gone. Her plump shapely calves
and bare feet. The others seemed smaller.

The ten thousand things narrow to three:
paper, ink, the brush's secret whisper
dragging its line. As my master promised
I have become an adept in surfaces,
a craft adrift in this floating world.

Mountain upon Mountain

Everything that lives yearns for children.
The wrestler gives his son extra helpings
of fish. The fox teaches her daughters
to dig. Where the pine cone falls, next year
we see a sturdy seedling beginning its climb.

I realize I have disappointed my unruly
offspring—my son the gambler, my grandson
drowning in rice wine and perfumed flesh.
Both my marriages failed. I forgive myself
the first. The second I should have spared.

Hiding from creditors, I sleep in an ancient hut
in the marshes north of the city. My publisher
shows me proofs when I creep to him at night
like a criminal. From the ruined doorway
I see the mountain, different in every light.

Our road is deserted, its ruts filled with grass.
When strangers stop, my clever daughter
(through whom I repay my unequal debt
to the generous world) serves them with tea.
She likes to read their fortunes in the leaves.

松山の
不二

The Mushroom Gatherers

I was born at the heart of the known world.
Another accident, my parents' poverty,
set me to work by the city's busiest bridge.
Around me, the swirl of whirlpools, eddies.
I was a twig, hurried along by the current.

How many addresses? Too many to count.
As soon as my neighbours learned my name
it was time to be gone. My friends believed
when the moment came to clean the floor
I preferred to pack my few things and move.

Solitude, my severe companion, never leaves.
She is at my shoulder now, in this retreat
among the reed-beds. In crowds, backstairs
at the theatre, or with the painted butterflies
of the green quarters, she steered my hand.

Her gaunt cousin Anonymity, a wraith
made of smoke, Poverty's brother, shadow
in the room's corner, always protected me
from adulation. I have changed my name
fifty times already, whenever I was known.

Was I given hard taskmasters? None harder
than myself. From their houses on the slopes
below the pine forests, villagers gather to hunt
for mushrooms. They gossip, tell tall tales,
the hours drift by. Some days I envy them.

Winter Wind

This day too blustery to draw, I sit
on the stump of a thousand-year tree
to see straw torn from the watchman's
hut, its peak laid bare like an outcrop.
Only a bird could cut through this wild air.

Three strangers pass. One, heavy laden,
carries a neatly furled umbrella, useless
in this gale. An old man and his servant
pause higher up. I notice the white cone
of the master's hat, his flying clothes.

A moment later, and the road is empty.
I am utterly alone. In the far distance
the mountain has drawn a shawl around
her shoulders. She has heard the forester
whistling a thin tune through his teeth.

Behind the Mountain

Scurry of sparrows in roof straw, hunting
stray grains. Memories jostle each other
under my unkempt thatch. I draw them
furiously, fast as they come. Only now
in my old age do I feel stirrings of skill.

Filling my pipe a moment ago, I saw
my aunt that distant farmyard day
winding silk on the rack, a few paces
toward me, then back, rhythm of work,
weary, I am sure, day drawing to a close.

Sweet smell of the hard-ridden horse
returned from market, Uncle scrubbing
its hot hindquarters, the horse's head
turned away from the attention, their
servant wrapping the saddle in its cloth.

And now it comes to me, the pungent
aroma of dried tobacco leaves, familiar
as horse dung, gleam of silk in sunlight,
sparrows in the closed morning glories,
the bucket where I saw my reflection.

The past is a sheet of polished bronze.
Colours, angles, flicker on it, flashes
of blinding light. Illusions, illusions.
I am still learning. Ten more years,
given time I may see like a sparrow.

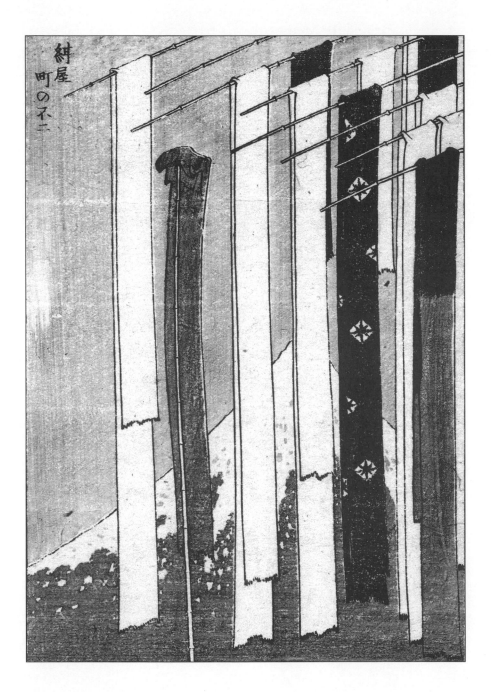

From the Dyers' Quarter

I teach my apprentices, day after
day, design is merely geometry,
circles, triangles, rectangles. And
the hand placing the last piece.
And then, what moved the hand.

Drawn from Life

He laid aside his short sword and flourished
the brushes over the blank sheet. One brush
for the drawing, one for the poem. Hunched
like a heron, he looked at the little shrine
and allowed the poem to introduce itself.

His three old servants were busy. One
was heating a flask of sake, one unpacking
the little box of food—rice cakes, as I recall—
the third wrapping a scroll in yellow silk.
In the marsh the reeds were stiff with frost.

An awakened eye. I see for the first time
the heron who waits for ever, the windblown
pine, the mountain. And the tired servants
intent on their tasks, the empty sky, my master
ready to defend us all with his short sword.

嶋田夕眺

夕陽不遠

Evening Sun on the River

Summer evenings I would wander down
to the hundred pilings breakwater, there
where the river bends. My fingers and arms
ached from the mirror-polishing, but I made
hundreds of drawings of that lazy scene.

This place at the northern edge of the city
was a favourite spot of anglers, fishing
for supper. The river, our stately guardian,
carries along the paper boats of our hopes,
dilutes our griefs and disappointments.

At this ancient haunt, I sketch the anglers
setting their lines. Their wives fan the coals
of little braziers, ready to broil the catch.
Under the cone of the shadowed mountain
the night fisherman hoists his black net.

Thunderstorm

I would have lived in such a village,
a dozen thatched roofs, a temple, one
street, the cherries in bloom, maple
leaves unfolding. From an indigo sky
lightning stabs between the houses.

In the street almost all the villagers
are caught in the storm. They cower
under the rain's fury, the lightning
strikes harmlessly, missing them all.
A pig roots casually in the garbage.

The mountain, white with new snow
rises above. O silk-robed goddess,
save me from bitterness. The dragon
swoops in on smoky wings, and dark
deeper than night dazzles my eyes.

Cutting Down a Tree

When I feel near the top of the mountain
I remember how much is still left to do.
At the age of six I was already obsessed
with the shape of things. In my fifties
everything I chose to draw was printed.

When I reached seventy I saw my work
was insignificant. Now at seventy-three
the forms of nature have begun slowly
to reveal themselves: how animals run,
how the old forester swings his axe.

By eighty I shall have improved in skill,
but not until ninety do I expect to see
into the heart of things. Ten years more,
and I hope to find my name enrolled
among the immortals in brush and ink.

At a hundred and ten, every least dot,
every line will be alive. Then, the old
tree will spring wild out of the page,
and the woodsmen cutting it. Those
who outlive me will see this magic.

大尾一筆
此不二

In a Single Stroke

The climb began in dark, before dawn,
finding a path through pines. The slope
was steep. Shortness of breath to the top.
No chance to pause at the crater, time
lashing you on. The descent will be hard.

Stonemason, Border Country

The others already
had the ship in harbour
tethering it with intertwined
hawsers of vine

He clung to the swaying mast
head bowed to the whirlwind
hammering into stillness
ancestral images

So the rabbit leaned his velvet head
at the greyhound's ear
the fiddler's bow
rested on the string

Corbel on Kilpeck Church (drawing by Enok Sweetland)

RAIN'S MANUSCRIPT

From the medieval Welsh of Dafydd ap Gwilym

Curiodd anwadal galon.
Cariad a wnaeth brad i'm bron.
Gynt yr oeddwn, gwn ganclwyf,
Yn oedd ieuenctid a nwyf,
Yn ddilesg, yn ddiddolur,
Yn ddeiliad cariad y cur,
Yn ddenwr gwawd, yn ddinych,
Yn dda'r oed, ac yn ddewr wych,
Yn lluniwr berw oferwaith,
Yn llawen iawn, yn llawn iaith,
Yn ddogn o bwynt, yn ddigardd,
Yn ddigri', yn heini'n hardd;

Ac weithian, mae'n fuan fâr,
Edwi 'dd wyf, adwedd afar,
Darfu'r rhyfig a'm digiawdd,
Darfu'r corff mau, darfer cawdd.
Darfu'n llwyr derfyn y llais,
A'r campau, dygn y cwympais.
Darfu'r awen am wenferch,
Darfu'r sôn am darfwr serch.
Ni chyfyd ynof, cof cerdd,
Gyngyd llawen ac angerdd,
Na sôn diddan am danun,
Na serch byth, onis eirch bun.

Flourishing in Wales between the lives of Dante and Chaucer, Dafydd overturned the conventions of courtly love, while bestowing immortality on his delight and torment, Morfydd. Ironic, self-mocking, intricate, his poems satirize the European inheritance from Catullus, Ovid, and the troubadours, in complex patterns of alliteration and rhyme (called in Welsh *cynghanedd*), whose rules he did much to codify. As with the poems of François Villon in the next century, only the bare shadow of his sardonic brilliance can be caught in English.

The Girls of Llanbadarn

Frustration, my old friend, pronounce
a plague on all Llanbadarn's girls.
I've paid the whole pack deep devotion
without reward, not a single smile,
from tender virgin (stern test of virtue)
young hussy, hag, or wanton wife.

Did I ever hesitate, or once hold back?
What slight could rate such weight of scorn?
How would she lose, that dark-eyed lass,
to seek me deep in the forest's centre?
What shame to dare that shaded den
loving me in my lair of leaves?

I dedicate from dawn till evening
to chants of love; I loose my charms
of primitive ancestral potency.
Each day I woo a dame or two.
My cruel lovers prove so gentle
they greet me like an enemy.

Each Sunday in Llanbadarn church
(judge if you will) I risk my soul,
turning my face to those fine tempters
and the nape of my neck to God's altar,
hidden behind my hat's brave feather,
perusing the pews with lingering lust.

Then a lively woman whispers low
to her winsome quick companion:
'See over there that whey-faced flirt
wearing his hair in curls like a girl?
I'd never risk such a roving lover,
that mischief-maker, scholar of sin.'

'You'd expect no better from this boy,'
murmurs the other behind her hand.
'He'll angle a lifetime for his answer.
Let him go hang, he's a giddy thing.'
A raw reward from that lovely lady,
for wild wooing a petty payment.

Must I say farewell to fair ones,
bidding adieu to all my dreams?
An outlaw lodged in a hermit's cell,
in a shady haven I'll hide my shame.
My lesson learned, my love days done,
I'll bury for good my backward glances.

I followed musicians, merry fellows.
Now I live solitary, sleep alone.

Tavern Trouble

One time I came to a singular town
(my faithful squire following on)
a sprightly town, a place to feast.
Being Welsh, accustomed to the best,
I lodged myself in a suitably fine
public inn, and ordered some wine.
I saw a shapely maiden there
in the tavern, my heart's desire,
cast my soul at the rising sun
of that slim delightful one.
Just for us two, I ordered a roast
and a good wine (not to boast).
Boys try anything. I called to see
if the shy girl would sit with me.
I'd only whispered, to be honest,
two magic words, before her breast
began to fill with love like mine.
I told the lively lass I'd find
my way to her (her raven hair)
once I heard snoring everywhere.
All were asleep. Now to my quest.
She and I were waking. Best
of my ambitions then entailed
reaching her bedside. They all failed.
I started badly, tumbling down,
clattering as I hit the ground.
A fallen fool gets to his feet
with greater clumsiness than speed.
I rose, but here the pains begin.
Rising, I caught (poor leg!) my shin
against the edge of a noisy stool,
where an ostler left it out, the fool.
Rising again, I failed to see
(fellow Welshmen, pity me)
where it had always been (I paid
for my impatience, I'm afraid)

in my stupidity I banged

    my forehead on the table end.

There was a basin there, of course,

    and a full-voiced bowl of brass.

The table fell, a heavy weight,

    both trestles, and the chairs to boot,

the brass bowl sang out after me

    so they could hear a mile away.

The basin yelled, my soul went dark,

    and all the dogs began to bark.

By the wall three Englishmen

    lay there in their stinking pen,

each one afraid to lose his pack.

    Their names? Dick, Jenkin, and Jack.

In clouded accents one of the three

    spoke to the others angrily:

'That's a Welshman over there,

    plotting mischief. Let's take care.

He'll steal our packs. Don't let him be.

    Look out! Stop thief! It's robbery!'

Now the ostler woke them all.

    Terrified, I hugged the wall.

Shouting threats, they groped around,

    searching every inch of ground.

Haggard, angry, scared to death,

    I blessed the dark and held my breath,

mumbling prayers, a fugitive,

    to save my abject skin and live.

And as my petty prayers were heard

    by God's good graces, undeterred,

sleepless, mortified, half dead,

    without reward I reached my bed.

It's good that saints are close. Perhaps

    God will forgive my little lapse.

The Mist

Yesterday (Thursday, my drinking day)
was a red-letter mark in the calendar.
I recovered my faith in women. Worn
wafer-thin with love, I was invited
to a love-tryst in the green cathedral,
a meeting made at my girl's choosing.

No man alive, under blaze of heaven,
knew of my pact with the shapely girl.
At sun's rising that Thursday morning
I leapt from bed brim full of laughter
and set my course to the small cottage
where the slim one was expecting me.

But now like a thief on the empty moor
a mist came creeping, a black cortège,
a parchment scroll, rain's manuscript,
clotted curds, a slippery hindrance,
a tin colander starting to rust through,
a fowling net on the swarthy soil.

A dark gate blocking a narrow path,
a winnowing sieve tossed up carelessly,
a monk's grey cowl shading the land,
darkening every vale and hollow,
a thorn fence bestriding the sky,
a purple bruise on the fogbound hill.

It was like wool, a thin veil of fleece
flimsy as smoke, a straw bonnet,
a hedge of rain barring my progress,
a coat of armour, a storm to soak me,
blinding my eyes so I was lost utterly,
a coarse cloak thrown over the county.

Then it was a castle right in my path,
hall of the fairy king, wind's territory,
a pair of fat cheeks chewing the earth,
torchbearers searching a pitchy sky
for its three pallid constellations,
a poet's blindfold, a bard's penalty.

A length of expensive cambric
thrown over the heavens, a halter
of spidery gossamer, French fabric,
on the moorland, fairies' realm,
a filmy breath of piebald smoke,
forest mist on a May morning.

Film on the eyes, a barking kennel,
ointment smeared on Hell's witches,
sodden dew become oddly sinister,
a discarded suit of damp chain-mail.
I'd sooner walk the pitch dark heath
than navigate this mist at noon.

At midnight stars light up the sky,
candles aflame in a dark chancel,
but this morning (bitter memory)
no moon, no stars, only a mist,
a prison door slammed behind me,
this mist, a misery past endurance.

Thus was my path curdled by clouds
leaving a stupefied stone-blind lover
stood stock-still, bereft of the sight
of Morfydd's elegant arching brows.

Forest Communion

Pure morning joy
under leafy canopy
at wake of day I heard

       the clever cock thrush
       pour his glittering song
       to melt the stoniest heart.

Sober-accented
foreign love-messenger
from as far as Carmarthen

       sent by my golden girl
       singing across borders
       right to this valley.

He wore a chasuble
speckled with mayflowers
fit for a celebrant

       his surplice the wind
       and on the altar
       the gleam of gold.

Morfydd sent him
this clever chorister
Mary's foster son

       singer of canticles
       pouring the gospel
       in every eager ear.

A leaf was raised
as consecrated host
while the slim nightingale

       in a nearby copse
       our valley poet
       trilled the sanctus bell.

Celebrating
in sight of God
our hedge-communion

       draining the loving-cup
       I relished that song
       and its green birthplace.

Old Age

My heart (vile traitor) began to fail, while
passions staged their own rebellion

      In a hundred disappointments,
      in the desire of youthful blood,
      in a tireless young man's vigour,
      in two hands manacled by love,
      in scant respect for poetry, robed
      in the shallow bravado of youth,
      in vanity's all-consuming mirror,
      in easy exchange of pleasantries,
      in health enough, a touch of fame,
      in laughter, grace, and elegance.

So now grown old I settle the score,
wrinkled and sad, waiting for death.

      Gone is my old familiar swagger,
      gone that vigour, and that passion,
      gone the rapid rush of language,
      gone my triumphs, and my failures,
      gone my verses made for Morfydd,
      gone hope of fame, all claims of conquests,
      gone recollection of my poems,
      gone all jesting, all desire gone,
      gone our gossip, our boasts of amours,
      gone all love. Unless she beckons.

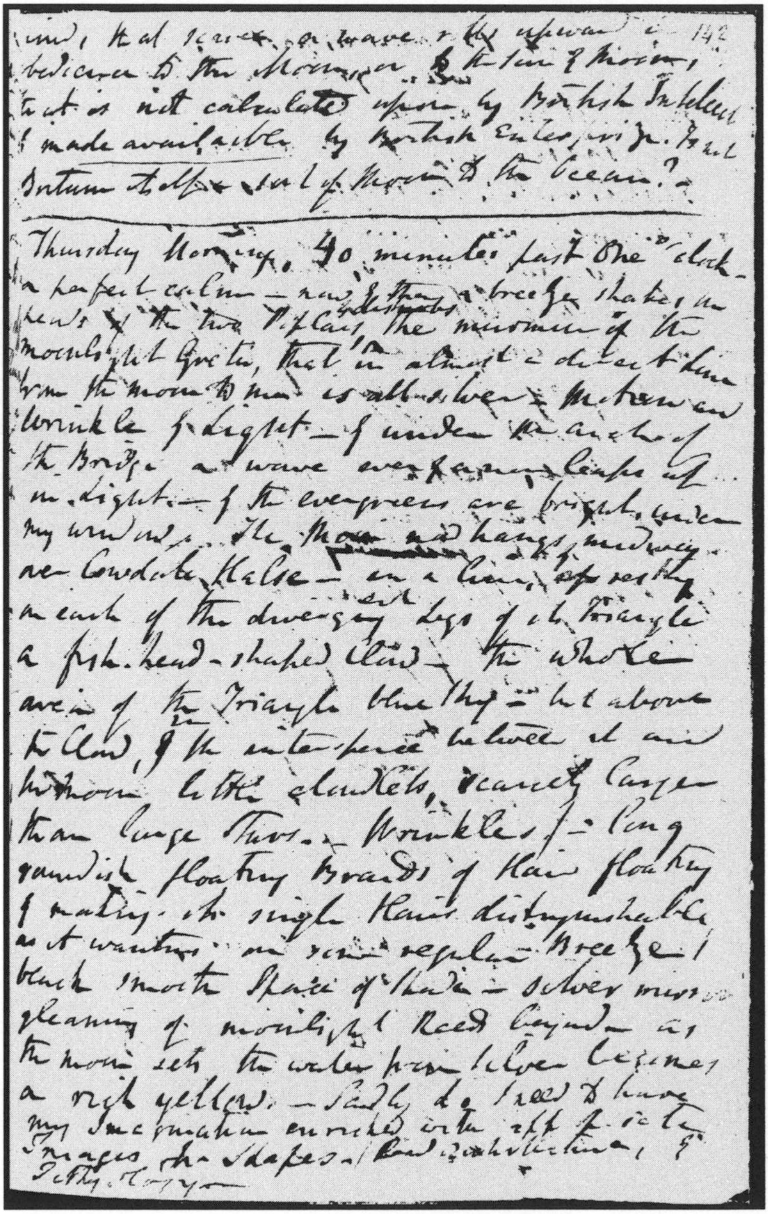
ind, that secret [illegible] wave [illegible] upward [illegible] 142
obedience to the Moon [illegible] the Sun & Moon,
that is not calculated upon by British Intellect
& made available by British Enterprize. Is not
Autumn itself a seal of Moon & the Ocean?

Thursday Morning, 40 minutes past One o'clock—
a perfect calm—now & then a breeze shakes the
heads of the two Poplars, the murmur of the
moonlight Greta, that in almost a direct line
from the moon to me is all silver—Motion and
Wrinkle of Light—& under the arch of
the Bridge a wave ever & anon leaps up
in light—& the evergreens are bright under
my window... The Moon hangs midway
over Cowdale Halse—in a line, apparently
on each of the diverging Legs of the Triangle
a fish-head-shaped Cloud—the whole
area of the Triangle blue sky—but above
the Cloud, & the interspace between it and
the Moon little cloudlets, scarcely larger
than large Stars—& Wrinkles, & long
roundish floating Braids of Hair floating
& waving—the single Hairs distinguishable
as it wanders in some regular Breeze—
black smooth Space of Shade—silver mass
gleaming of moonlight Reed beyond—as
the moon sets the water from below becomes
a rich yellow.—Sadly do I need to have
my Imagination enriched with [illegible]
Images & Shapes & Recollections, &
Poetry [illegible]

Coleridge, Notebook 21, folio 73 (see page 129)

THE LOW VOICE OF QUIET CHANGE

Recoveries from S T Coleridge

Bristol, London, Göttingen and Keswick
December 1797 - November 1803

Notebook 21, a small octavo volume in red leather, was given to Samuel Taylor Coleridge by his Bristol publisher Joseph Cottle on December 6, 1797. A desk memorandum book rather than a pocket-book, it accompanied the poet to Germany the following year, to the Lake District in 1800, and to Malta in 1804, with a final entry in February 1805. It can now be read at the British Library, where most of Coleridge's seventy or so notebooks reside.

The notebooks recorded the poet's fleeting thoughts and perceptions when he was not engaged on his major poems. Notebook 21, the third of his journals, is notable in its early pages for detailed nature notes, the late-night refuge of a poet increasingly plagued by self-doubt. The Malta journey was intended to restore Coleridge to good health and productivity, but the notebooks reveal a deep sense of loneliness, though there is no falling-off in alert observation and wry humour. More than anything, they record the intricate movement of one of literature's liveliest intellects, who in this journal was the first to use the word 'unconscious' for the hidden workings of the mind.

Many of the entries in this notebook were included in Ernest Hartley Coleridge's *Anima Poetae*, the 1895 selection of the poet's prose. More recently, all the journals have been transcribed and edited by Kathleen Coburn in a monumental series of volumes, and Giles Goodland has made excellent use of these materials in his 1998 *Overlay*. The current fragments are recovered from Notebook 21, in chronological order, adding nothing. I have made cuts, to reveal the poetry on every page of the journal. Given his delight in experiments of all kinds, scientific, social and linguistic, it is possible that Coleridge would give an ironic welcome to these poems recovered from the great quarry of his private meditations.

[1]

Such light as Lovers love—
                Moon behind Cloud
        Emerging to make the Blush visible
                                the long Kiss kindled

All our notions
        husked in phantasms of Place & Time
                still escape the finest sieve & Winnow of our Reason

Severity of Winter—the King's-fisher
                                slow short flight
                        observe all its colours
                                almost as if a flower

        Poetry gives most pleasure
                        when only generally
                                & not perfectly understood

[2]

The nightingales in a little wood of blossomed Trees
    singing—and a bat
            wheeling incessantly—

                noise of Frogs
        not unpleasant—spinning wheels
                in a large manufactury

Starlings in vast Flights, like smoke
    now circular, inclined
        now a Square—now a Globe—
            Ellipse—then oblongated Balloon with Car suspended

            expanding, condensing
                glimmering and shivering
                    thickening, deepening, blackening!

[3]

the Lute's delicious fingering

Was this the Flower of all thy voluminous Papers
                         Folios predestined to no better end
        than to make winding sheets
                         in Lent
                                 for Pilchards

[4]

Slanting pillars of misty light

A day of clouds & threatening Showrlets
                                 No sun
            no absolute gleam
                         but the mountains in & beyond Borrodale
                                 bright & *washed*—
the crag such a very gloomy purple
                 its treeage such a very black green

                     The thin scattered rain-clouds
                             scudding
             a visible interspace

                             the crescent Moon
                     hung, and partook not
                                 of the motion

         her own hazy Light fill'd up the concave
                                 as if painted
                     & the colors had run

[5]

prismatic colours transmitted from the Tumbler—

Wordsworth came—I talked with him—

beauteous spectra of two colors
orange
violet—
green
Peagreen & then *grew* a beautiful moss
the same on the mantle-piece at Grasmere—

abstract Ideas—
& unconscious Links!

[6]

The soil rich, dark Mould
                    Stratum of tenacious Clay
        foundation of Rocks
                    lifting their back above the Surface

            The Trees gigantic Black Oak
                            Magnolia
                                Fraxinus excelsior
                Platane
                        & a few stately Tulip Trees—

I applied this by a fantastic analogue
                to Wordsworth's Mind
        March 26 1801
                                Fagus exaltata sylvatica

The spring with the little cone of loose sand
                ever rising & sinking at the bottom
            surface without a wrinkle

            Northern Lights remarkably fine
                    a purple blue / in shooting pyramids—

Draw out the secrets from men's Hearts
        as Egyptian Enchanters by Strains of Music
                draw serpents from their lurking places—

                I am sincerely glad
            he has bidden farewell to all small Poems—
                    & is devoting himself to his great work—

                now he is at the Helm of a noble Bark—
        it is all open Ocean
                    & a steady Breeze

[7]

Oct. 19. 1803.
           tomorrow my Birth Day
                   31 years of age!
O me! This *year*
        one painful Dream /
              I have done nothing!

all hearts anxious concerning Invasion—

        A grey Day, windy—
                  Sun in slanting pillars
           illuminated parcels of mist
    now racing
        now slowly gliding
    now stationary/

        why have I not an unencumbered Heart!

              Books the deep reservoir
   my mind so populous, so active
           this heart so filled with affections—
why for years not one Delight
          rings sharp to the Beat of the Finger—

        But still said to the poetic Feeling when it awak'd
        Go!—
              come tomorrow—

Storm all night

[8]

        murmur of moonlight Greta all silver
    Motion and Wrinkle & Light
& under the arch of the Bridge
    a wave ever & anon leaps up in Light
& the evergreens are bright, under my window

    The Moon now hangs midway
& on the Legs of its Triangle a fish-head-shaped Cloud
    above the Cloud little cloudlets
scarcely larger than large Stars—

        Wrinkles /—
  silver mirror /
gleaming of moonlight Reeds beyond—
        as the moon sets
  the water from Silver
    becomes a rich yellow—

Sadly do I need to have my Imagination enriched
    with appropriate Images for Shapes—

  Read Architecture
    & Ichthyology—

[9]

As it entered the Fish's Head, the Moon
                    barred & cross-barred, over its whole face
            became a shapeless, or perhaps unshapely, Lump /—

                    the Greta now
                            only a grey Gleamer!—

before the Moon reached the Hill
            was a space of Blue, only half its length
                    it emerged, half in brightness /
                            and sank
                    in thinner & thinner Slips of Light

                    just at the last
            a strong Likeness of a Sheep on the Mountain
                            head & all!

                    So passes Night
                            & all her favors vanish

[10]

The Voice of the Greta
and the Cock-crowing:

the Voice seems to grow, like a Flower
on or about the water beyond the Bridge
while the Cock crowing is any place I imagine

The Moon, now waned to a perfect Ostrich's Egg
hangs over our House almost—
The Sky covered
with whitish & dingy *Cloudage*
thin dingiest Scud close under the moon
one side of it moving
all else moveless
The water leaden white

& the Moon is gone
The Cock-crowing too has ceased
The Greta sounds on, for ever

But I hear only
the Ticking of my Watch
in the Pen-place of my Writing Desk
& the far lower note of the Fire—

perpetual
yet seeming uncertain /

it is the low voice of quiet change
of Destruction
doing its work
by little
& little

[11]

the 7 Stars
    and all the rest in the height of Heaven bedimmed
        those on the descent
                bright & frosty—

    the river a loud voice
        self-biographer of today's rains & thunder showers—

                The owls silent

O after what a day of distempered Sleeps
        all sense of Time utterly lost /
            fever, rheumatic pain

                I get up / am calm

    looked out at the Sky
        thought it all dark
            but looked again

    & there were many Stars
        so dim and *dingy*
with hollow rays, tube-like as Hairs
        ensheathing Light & Heat
          producing cold & darkness

[12]

Midnight

I had taken a considerable Quantity of λαυδανυμ

closed my eyes

instantly appeared a spectrum, of a Pheasant's Tail
that altered
into round wrinkly shapes like Horse dung
still more like baked Apples, brought in after Dinner

went to the window to empty my Urine-pot
grandeur of the View

1 darkness
2 grey-blue steely Glimmer
of the Greta, & the Lake
3 The black
form preserving Mountains
4 the Sky
moon-whitened there
cloud-blackened here
the Horizon grey-white
the space between my eye & the Lake
one formless Black

Moon descending
two Nights more than a Half moon
set behind the black point
fitted *itself on to it,* like a Cap of Fire—
became a crescent /
then a mountain of Fire in the Distance /
then the Peak itself on fire—
one steady flame—
& vanishing
up boiled
a swell of Light—

215 216

217 218

George Catlin: Four Cherokees (1841)

from CHEROKEE RELICS

The Journals and Poems of Adam Daniel
known to the Cherokees as White Raccoon

for Ramona

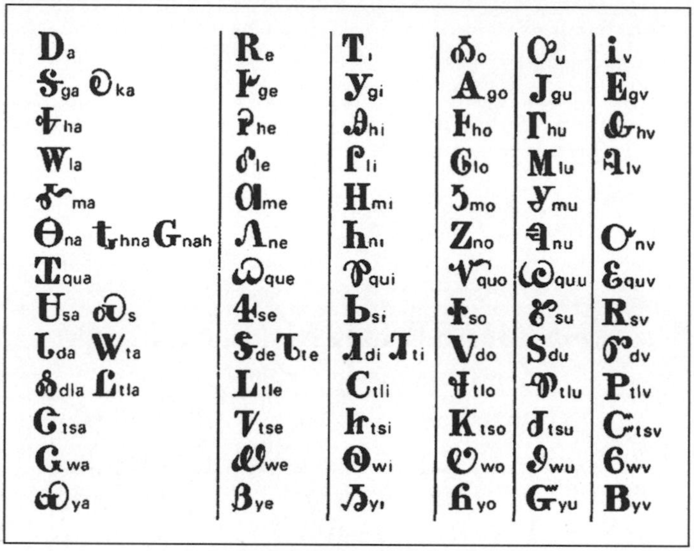

a	e	i	o	u	v
D a	R e	T i	Ꭳ o	Ꮕ u	i v
Ꮜ ga Ꮎ ka	F ge	y gi	A go	J gu	E gv
Ꮏ ha	P he	� hi	F ho	Γ hu	hv
W la	Ꮮ le	P li	G lo	M lu	Ꮈ lv
ma	Ꭴ me	H mi	mo	y mu	
Ꮎ na hna G nah	Λ ne	h ni	Z no	nu	O nv
T qua	Ꮖ que	P qui	V quo	Ꮗ quu	E quv
U sa Ꮝ s	4 se	b si	so	su	R sv
L da W ta	de te	di ti	V do	S du	dv
dla Ꮭ tla	L tle	C tli	tlo	tlu	P tlv
G tsa	V tse	tsi	K tso	J tsu	C tsv
G wa	we	Ꭼ wi	wo	wu	6 wv
ya	B ye	yi	yo	G yu	B yv

Sequoyah's Cherokee syllabary

Late in 1838, by order of President Andrew Jackson, the entire tribe of the Cherokees was removed under armed guard from their home in the Smoky Mountains to the territory now known as Oklahoma. The Removal followed the discovery of a nugget of gold in a stream flowing out of Cherokee land, but there were no further finds; the Indians were settled in a part of Oklahoma rich in oil — the final irony.

The experiences of Adam Daniel are based in part on those of John Burnett, whose account of the Trail of Tears is preserved in Cherokee, North Carolina, along with the Army roll-call of Indians taken on the Trail.

I. BEFORE DAWN IN THE FOREST

A new life

Today it seems I began my life over

Before dawn in the forest
no light, no warmth
huge pale mushrooms, grown overnight
gazed up like the faces of dead men
and the trees were petrified giants

Dawn came slowly, bringing colour
deep green branches
and (almost hidden among leaves)
the smoky blue huckleberries that I was hunting

I turned to pick the berries
and found I was not alone
Behind me in a half-circle
Indians
silent statues
their breath frosting on the air

They beckoned me with friendly gestures
and without a struggle
with no word spoken
I became one of them

Back at their camp
the old men gave me a new name:
Wapasabanah, or White Raccoon

Next week I shall be sixteen
but by then I may be past birthdays
grown to a man

Dear God
what will become of me ?

Song about the white boy

Skinny wrists and skinny ankles
what shall we do with him ?

Face as white as a pigeon feather
what name shall we give him ?

He scurries about like a scared raccoon
what can we make of him ?

Let the boy come hunting and eat our food
and put some flesh
on those skinny wrists and skinny ankles.

In the council-chamber

In the morning they took me to their council-chamber
and placed me in front of the chief :

'This is Wapasabanah
he is skinny
but we make him one of us.'

This set everyone laughing
then one of the old men took my arm
and led me to where each tribe sat
naming them:
Wild Potato, Bird, Long Hair
Blue, Paint, Deer and Wolf.
And a boy about my age called out:
'Let him be a Wild Potato.'

And again they laughed, and I joined in the joke
then they turned to more important business.

Question

My parents think me dead

One word
and they would take me from here

Who cast the spell
that has struck me dumb?

Encounter

I went to the cave alone

The stalactites moved in the torchlight
but they had no eyes

I found Rainmaker in a trance
the floor covered with bones

You will be my son, he said.

Rainmaker's tasks

The seasons come like distant relatives
visit with us a few months, then leave
Rainmaker tells us how to use them
when to sow and when to harvest

Rainmaker is a great magician
he can fly underground

The stars circle above us constantly
giving direction to our hunting-trails
Rainmaker can read our success in them
and in the moon's face as she fattens and starves

Rainmaker is a great magician
he can fly underground

And when the sun strikes the crops
and the rivers run dry
he prays for rain, and the rain comes
or he fails, and then we kill him.

Rainmaker's jaguar mask

. Rainmaker has masks

When one of us is sick
he comes in the shape of an old witch
and mumbles spells
through toothless gums

At every marriage
Rainmaker is the sly smiler
leading the revelry
and whispering in the bride's ear

When we need rain he is a swallow
flying low over the ground
then he walks out of his house
and the first drop falls into his palm

But when we prepare for war
he runs out headed like Jaguar
black spots stamped on yellow hair
his nostrils and eyes flame red

Bristles sprout from his eyebrows and cheeks
he bares his curbed white teeth
and the girls run indoors shrieking
then the little boys

And all the cats in the village
stand on tiptoe
every hair on end
then back away spitting

While behind the mask Rainmaker laughs
to see his magic work.

Little Squirrelfoot's first whisky

The pit of my belly
where the fire-water went
burns like a torch at night
with red and yellow sparks

The top of my head
is spinning slowly
My head is a sycamore leaf
caught in a whirlpool

There is a black bear watching me
from the other side of the river
He is dancing
his knees stamp up and down
his head is wagging from side to side
and he smiles to me in friendship

The earth and moon and trees are watching me
my knees stamp up and down
If this is what it feels like, being a bear
I want to be a bear.

Midsummer night

You are asleep. Your skin
is the stretched surface of water
drawn tight by the full moon rising

The cold light strikes from your thighs
and the polished curve of your shoulder
till all my bones glow red-hot

I am at the mercy of my bones
until they are plunged, hissing
deep in that icy lake.

Full Moon Rising

I met my girl
by Falling Water River

I met my wife
the magician's daughter

The charm is woven
by Falling Water River

She weaves the charm
the magician's daughter.

Crossing the river

This swift water
tumbles the stones

The stones when they fall
shatter to pebbles

The pebbles grow smooth
for the darting trout

The trout are the souls
that will swim in the river

The hurrying river
that runs to the grave

Sang Little Terrapin
putting his feet down carefully.

On the trail

I am learning to walk silently
by treading in the others' footsteps

But still the twigs crack
and they make me carry each broken twig

Yesterday when we made camp
my left hand was full

They counted them gravely
and laid them out side by side:

'In enemy country
each of these is a dead Cherokee.'

2. THE TRIBES

Wild Potato

Long, long ago
our friends in Virginia tell us
an Englishman came there

And took away with him
a tobacco plant
and a wild potato

Two such ordinary things
they seemed unimportant
at the time.

Bird

You hold it in your hand
open your hand
it does not fall

This is magic

Indeed
when you held it in your hand
it was a stone.

Long Hair

At the creek in sunshine

The gnarled old women
rubbing clothes on rocks
with knotted hands

But one girl dips her hair
and flings it forward
like a bright waterfall
tumbling over her breasts

And stands there
lonely as a willow.

Blue

This perfect bowl
at the forest's centre

Huge thumb-print
of Rainmaker's ancestor

Full to the brim
with clear sky water

A drop from the lake
mounted in silver

Hangs round the neck
of Rainmaker's daughter.

Paint

Slender stalks
each with a fine plume
dipped in crimson

Indian paint-brush
swaying gently
alongside the trail

Valuable in a crisis
like war
or first love.

Deer

Buckskin over my shoulder
my head horned
sockets filled with buckeyes

Once two hunters stalking a herd
shot each other
and died bewildered

I am dancing your death dance, brother Deer

Running in circles, leaping and bounding
I raise my head to sniff the air
the arrow enters my throat suddenly.

Wolf

I remember the great war
when the Creeks captured one of our warriors
and gave him to their women

They burnt the soles of his feet
put grains of corn under the blisters
then told him to dance

So he began singing his death song
and soon the women were laughing and clapping their hands
as he stamped about the fire in wider and wider circles

Till he was dancing right at the edge of the darkness
then he gave a loud cry and disappeared into the trees
and when his feet gave out he was still free

He crawled into a hollow log and slept
and all night a wolf licked the soles of his feet
so that by morning the pain had gone

This was how it was each day till he reached home
and I remember, years later, how some nights
I would hear him call into the darkness

And how I listened for the answering howl
echoing out of the forest
then my father would come back to the tent and sleep.

3. FORMULAS

Formula

I see my words
I see my words

My words fly through the air
feathered like birds
My words fly through the air
feathered like arrows

They find the birds in air
They bring them down

I hold my words

They are sharp
like claws
They are hard
like arrowheads

Like pebbles thrown into water

My words fly through the air
they fly through the air echoing.

To make the best medicine

The leaves turn red
the leaves are on fire, they turn red
they drop into the river

The wild plum leaf falls slowly
there is no hurry
the hickory leaf falls slowly
the river is waiting to carry it down
the dogwood leaf falls slowly

When the sweet sassafras leaf falls
the river is waiting to carry it down

This is good medicine now.

Before hunting

Give me the wind
I feel it on my face

You, great Hunter
great River hunting through the earth
I come to the foam at the water's edge
I touch your spittle

You are covered with leaves
the leaves are red with blood
the blood of my prey runs into your blood
now you are pleased

Give me the wind

You, old red Fire
hover over me while I sleep
give me good dreams

The trails go everywhere
the leaves are red with blood

I cook my prey
you bury it in your stomachs
you Water, you Fire.

For catching catfish

Listen to me, you listen to me
see you swim into white water
moving about together like one fish
you Blue Cat I throw you food
you catch it now.

To find a lost hog

Suspend an ancient arrowhead by a string
(a quartz pebble will do as well)
and say to it:

Hey brown pebble, you listen to me
you told me no lies before
now I am hunting my lost hog
you find it for me
White Raccoon

Then swing the stone and look where it points

If you do not find the hog
there will always be some good reason.

4. STORIES

First story

There was a time
when the whole world was covered with ice
and all the bears were white

You don't believe me
nobody believes this story.

How the mountains were made

At the beginning of things
it was like making a pot

The Great Spirit took a lump of earth
and set it spinning
smoothing it with his hand until it was round

And when he stopped
the water from his hand sat in the cracks and hollows
and trickled down all over
But later, after his hands were dry
he wanted to touch his new toy one last time
and where he rested his fingers
the sticky clay jumped up into ridges and conical hills
and the warmth of his hand covered them with trees

And that is where we live.

Totem

One of our Cherokee ancestors
wanting to carve a woman
chose a slender sapling
straight-limbed and smooth as a baby
marked it and watched it grow
till he liked its curves
then he felled the tree
stood it upright and looked it over

She was perfect.
He took his flint axe to make her eyes
but it sprang back from the young wood
and his wrist ached.
He left the figure in a corner and turned his back on it.

He started again on a redwood.

As the flint caressed its sides
wolves, bears and eagles
possums and marmosets, prairie dogs and buffalo
ranged up and down the bursting trunk
jostling for room.

The noises deafened him and scared him suddenly.
He threw some blazing thorns around its base.
It burned with a clear blue flame
and the splitting wood sang in the heat.

He recognized the voice
and tried to snatch her from the fire
but scorched his hands.
He is still there
waiting to bury the ashes.
The tree is still singing.

Jack Coldweather's dream

I dreamed I made my way to the Blue Lake
which our ancestors knew about
but never found
where wounded creatures that escape the hunter
go to be cured

And while I lay there on the bank
Stag came with an arrow in his side
he plunged into the lake and swam across
climbed out and shook himself
and trotted away without a scar

Then other animals, Raccoon, Opossum
Wild Turkey and old man Bear
came and were cured in just the same way

At last old Grandfather Hare came hopping
filled with malice
looked with his evil eye
at the brimming bowl
then he tipped it with his foot
and in seconds the whole lake drained away

The forest is full of animals now
leaping and running in terror

They have run out of my nightmare

I cannot tell what is in store for the Cherokees
but I am afraid.

Poem for the children of our children

Listen! Since the beginning of time
the Cherokees had their home in the mountains
between the ocean and the Mississippi:
Hiwassee, Sugar Town, Quaratchi, Tugaloo
Chilhowee, Burning Town
Echota, Tellico and Tannassee

And first of all the Spaniards discovered us
but all they wanted was gold
and they found none
so we shook hands with them and they went away

Next there was a great noise of drums
and the British came marching through in their red coats
so they discovered us
they brought us news from their Great King
and made maps with the message:
CHEROKEE NATION
and some of our chiefs went to London
and shook the people's hands

Then the Americans discovered us
and while we were shaking hands with them
they were giving our lands fresh names:
Georgia, Virginia, Carolina
and the maps had a new message on them:
LANDS CLAIMED BY THE CHEROKEES

From that time things were different.

5. WASHINGTON TALK

Letter to President Jackson

September 1834

Dear Andy

The situation here is critical

It seems the gold nugget was washed down
out of the Cherokee claim
this is already no secret in Georgia

You understand my position
I have the militia on hand
but the people are arming themselves

The South cannot afford another disturbance

Will   Wilson Lumpkin
                                        Governor
                                        State of Georgia

Letter to Wilson Lumpkin

10 November 1834

Dear Will

I've said it before:
build a fire under them

When it gets hot enough
they'll move

Andy   Andrew Jackson
                                        President

Appointment

For the Removal of the Cherokees
to Indian Territory
West of the Mississippi

Commissioners
William Carroll, Tennessee
Wilson Lumpkin, Georgia

By me
this seventh day of June 1836
Andrew Jackson
President of the United States

The last word

After much thought
the Supreme Court pronounced the Removal
unconstitutional

Jackson had this to say:

John Marshall has made his decision
now let him enforce it.

6. EXTRACTS FROM THE JOURNAL

November 5 1838 *Entering Meigs County*
My wife's birthday. The rain still falling. Our senses dulled, we move through the dripping forest like ghosts, dumb and purposeless. Perhaps tomorrow when we awake we shall feel some sense of catastrophe.

December 6 *Robertson's Road, Montgomery Co.*
Through Springfield yesterday on our way to the Kentucky line. Last night encamped to the east of Clarksville in the woods above Red River. They say this was an old Indian hunting-ground, and our conversation on the subject, together with the howling of some dogs in the darkness, may well have caused my strange dream. It seemed, as the bonfire burned lower, that figures appeared in the smoke, Cherokees recently buried beside the trail. Burnt Tobacco came, and Jack Coldweather, the tattoo-scars slashed across their faces like veins of silver and copper, their feet rising and falling silently. I saw Horse Fly with his head thrown back, and the crimson paint gleaming on his body. I saw his mouth open to howl, but no sound came. Then there were others whose names I had forgotten, the sweat glistening on their cheek-bones. There were a number of disconnected images—a mass of hair flew up and settled slowly, and a pair of eyes rested on me for a moment so that I caught my breath. Then a hand was thrust out and snatched mine. I remember most vividly the firelight warm on my face, as I joined the dance.

December 16 *Joy, Kentucky*
When we leave each stopping-place the trail behind us is littered with all the debris of a retreating army. The luxuries are abandoned first, the rocking-chairs and heavy beds that have made the wagons of the rich into travelling homes, and then the steel trunks and valises full of silk dresses, writing-desks with cunningly concealed drawers, cases of cosmetics and perfumes; today we passed the remains of a travelling library, its contents ransacked, no doubt for liquor, and spilling out into the snow.

I confess that I paused at this find for more than a few minutes, looking into the leathery volumes, tempted even by the feel of their bindings; but in the end I had to remind myself that I could no more afford to carry than could their original owner. One volume, however, I was unable to resist, Jonathan Swift's account of the travels of Lemuel Gulliver, printed in London. I stood in the snow, reading five or six pages, and found at once a man after my own heart. He would surely have appreciated the name of the town where we encamped tonight.

Tomorrow, if not too hampered by floating ice, we are to cross the Ohio, the 'Beautiful River'.

December 25   *Willard's Landing*

The Mississippi, end of our world. Across the river unknown forests, unknown hills and valleys, and beyond them the names of tribes, Osage, Kansa, Iowa, Missouri. Then the prairies.

And today is Christmas Day; thoughts of the cold stable in Bethlehem. The Landing is the gathering-place for many of the earlier parties, halted by the frozen river. Jesse Bushyhead, here with his sister Susan, held a great congregation at which he preached on the theme of Joy. All our blessings named, one by one, our friends, our faith, even the journey itself. This sermon will save many lives—a stratagem, no doubt, but one that a saint might contrive.

After the service I walked with him along the river bank. It is marked in places with steep cliffs of rock, some of them arched and colonnaded like ancient temples. This whole area is honeycombed with lead mines, and the inhabitants use these rock formations for shot towers. They pour the molten lead through sieves, and the drops fall through the air, cooling into musket balls to keep us on the other side of the river. We spoke of these and other things without rancour, our hearts too full of hope to indulge in malice. Jesse even smiled when telling me of Junaluska's comment at the start of the Removal. The old chief, who had saved Jackson's life at the Horseshoe Bend, was sent to Washington to plead with him, but the President refused to meet his old friend. 'If I had known of this at Horseshoe Bend,' said Junaluska, 'history would have been written differently.'

Jesse reports eighty-two deaths in his company, but thinks the worst may be behind us.

December 30   *Across the Mississippi*

Encamped on the west bank. As we were putting up the tents I fell into conversation with John Burnett, a private in McClellan's Company of the mounted infantry. He was wearing no shirt, and I found that he had given it to a Cherokee mother to wrap around her baby. There was something in his face that stirred memories, and at last, seeing my bewilderment, he laughed and told me that he had often hunted with the Cherokees in his youth, and after saving the life of one of their boys had visited them frequently on the most friendly of terms. He knew me, but only by my Indian name, and was amused to hear my story. We talked well into the night. As he left my tent, the coat over his shoulders barely protecting him from the cold night air, I found running through my head one item from the list of trading prices which was nailed to the door-post of the store: One Shirt, one Beaver Skin, in season. Strange how the chance of fate can alter our valuations: One Shirt, one Beaver Skin, one Cherokee baby.

January 7   *Across the St Francis River*

Last night I dreamed that I was in a huge cave hung with stalactites, the walls covered with paintings, where I saw a multitude of familiar faces. There was Full Moon Rising, a young girl, just as she looked when I first saw her by the water's edge, and the wise old face of Rainmaker her father; there was Little Squirrelfoot, drunk, dancing clumsily, and my good friend Little Terrapin, the poet, day-dreaming. On the other wall were long-forgotten faces, my family, dressed for Sunday morning service; my father's tall stovepipe hat, my mother's black silk shawl, the children's shining faces, mine among them. I turned to the cave mouth and saw a great black bear filling the entrance. He took me by the hand (his hard claws in my palm) and led me out into blinding sunlight.

6. WORDS IN THE DARK

The death of Jack Coldweather

They made a bed of birch branches
covered it with furs and skins
and laid him on it.

When he smiled
the skin stretched tight across his jaw.
They waited for the end.

Suddenly he got to his feet.

'Listen to this story.
When I was a little boy
I kept a tortoise tied to a post by its hind leg.
As the days passed the rope grew rotten
until in the end it broke, and the tortoise
slowly, step by step, made its way to the woods.'

Then he lay down again
and died soon afterwards.

They closed his eyes
covered his bright face with the death mask
and went away slowly, step by step.

19 November 1838

Little Sparrow

The daughter of Crying Wolf
and Katie Nettlecarrier

Born on the Trail of Tears
and lived four days

A little sparrow
fallen from the nest

14 December 1838

Burnt Tobacco

An American soldier, John Burnett
tells of his boyhood in the Smoky Mountains
'hunting the deer, the wild boar
and the timber wolf'
and how in 1828 an Indian boy
sold a gold nugget to a white trader
which sealed the doom of the Cherokees.

When the prospectors moved in
Burnett was in the regiment that drove his friends
along the Trail of Tears to Indian Territory:

'In the chill
of a drizzling rain of an October morning
I saw them loaded like cattle or sheep
into six hundred and forty-five wagons.

Each name tells a story:
Crying Wolf, Jack Coldweather and White Raccoon
Tom Nettlecarrier, Burnt Tobacco
Sweet Water, Little Terrapin and Stump
Eight out of four thousand dead.

The evening comes with its shadows
and the mists rising thick along the mountain ridges
might be smoke from the pipes
of four thousand silent Indians.

I am reminded
of Burnt Tobacco and his family of five
dead, along with the deer
the wild boar and the timber wolf.'

30 December 1838

A Rainbow strangely preserving it's form
on broken clouds, with here a bit out, here
a bit in, & yet still a rainbow even as
you might place bits of colored ribbons at
distances so as still to preserve the form
of a Bow to the mind. Dec. 25. 1804—

There are two sorts of talkative fellows, whom
it would be injurious to confound/ & I, S. T.
Coleridge, am the latter. The first sort is of
those who use five hundred words more
than needs to express an idea—that is
not my case—few men, I will be bold to
say, put more meaning into their words
than I or choose them more deliberately
& discriminatingly. The second sort is
of those who use five hundred more
ideas, images, reasons &c than there
is any need of to arrive at their
object/ till the only object arrived at
is that the sordid mind's eye of
the bye stander is dazzled with colors
succeeding so rapidly as to leave one
vague impression that there has been
a great blaze of colors all about
something. Now this is my case—& a
grievous fault it is/ my illustrations
swallow up my thesis—I feel too

Coleridge, Notebook 21, folio 121ᵛ (see pages 166–7)

SOME BUSINESS OF AFFINITY

Recoveries from S T Coleridge

Malta, December 1804 - January 1805

[1]

A brisk Gale
spots of foam
peopled the *alive* Sea

combined with white Sea Gulls it seemed
the foam spots had taken Life and Wing
& flown up

One travels along with the Lines of a mountain—/
I wanted, years ago
to make Wordsworth sensible of this—/

Keswick Vale
repose?
My Soul lies & is quiet
upon the broad level vale—

would it act?
it darts into the mountain Tops
like a Kite
& like a chamois goat
runs along the Ridges

like a Boy that makes a sport on the road
running along a wall
or narrow fence

[2]

Nature, an ever industrious Penelope
          for ever unravelling what she had woven
    for ever weaving
        what she had unravelled

                A Rainbow
                    strangely
              preserving its form
        on broken clouds
      with here a bit out
    here a bit in
        & yet
still a rainbow

[3]

two sorts of talkative fellows

The first
use five hundred words more than needs—
not my case—

The second
five hundred more ideas, images, reasons &c
till the mind's eye of the bye-stander
is dazzled
with a great Blaze of colours

this is my case—
& a grievous fault it is /
my illustrations swallow up my thesis

I feel too intensely omnipresence
all in each
platonically speaking—
or psychologically

my brain-fibres
or the spiritual Light which abides in the brain marrow
as visible Light appears to do
in sundry rotten mackerel & other *smashy* matters

is of too general affinity with all things /
and tho' it perceives the *difference* of things
yet is eternally pursuing the likenesses

[4]
                        thinking of Brain & Soul
what we know of an embryo—
                    one particle combines with another
                            & so lengthens & thickens—

might make a very amusing Allegory
                        of an embryo Soul up to Birth!

                        Try! it is promising!—
            You have not above 300 volumes to write
                & as you write a volume once in ten years
                        you have ample Time
                                my dear Fellow!
Never be ashamed of scheming—
                    look at the bright side always—

The survey of this pocket book might suggest
                a passionate address to my Lamp or Tapers
                        forms so often gazed at
                    sometimes frightened of perpendicular
                                by my groans

        do *think* of it
                        not merely dream—
            O by & by

[5]

I have been always preyed upon by some Dread
    perhaps all my faulty actions consequence
 of some Dread or other on my mind /
    fear of Pain, or Shame, not prospect of Pleasure /

So in Boyhood
    imaginary fears of the Itch in my Blood /
     a short-lived Fit of Fears from sex—

then horror of DUNS
   & a state of struggling with madness
      from an incapability of hoping
    I should be able to marry Mary Evans
       had all the effects of direct Fear
& I have lain for hours awake at night, groaning & praying—

Then came that stormy time /
    for a few months America inspired Hope
   & I became an exalted Being—
     then Rob. Southey's alienation /
 my marriage—
   constant dread respecting Mrs Coleridge's Temper, &c

finally stimulants
   in the fear & prevention of violent Bowel-attacks
    from mental agitation /
        night-horrors /
since then every error immediate effect of the Dread
     of these most shocking Dreams
   any thing to prevent them /
    all this interwoven with minor consequences—
  the juice between the cherries in a cherry pie /
    procrastination in dread
& something else in consequence of that procrast. &c /

[cont.]

from the same cause
the least langour in a Letter from S. H.
drives me wild /

& it is most unfortunate that I
so fearfully despondent
should have concentered my soul thus
on one almost as feeble in Hope

[6]

This Evening the most perfect Halo
   circling the roundest and brightest moon I ever beheld—
           so entire a circle
                    it gave the whole
              the moon included
        the appearance of a solid body—
                      an enormous Planet /
   the Moon a small circular bason of fluid
        that still more copiously emitted light
            the interspatial area equally substantial
                        but sullen /

thence I meditate on magnitude

        why do I seek for mountains
    when in the flattest countries the Clouds present
        so much more romantic & *spacious* forms
 & the coal-fire
    so much more varied?

            do I not
        more or less consciously
           fancy myself a Lilliputian
   to whom these would be mountains—

my pleasure being playful
    a voluntary poem in *hieroglyphics*

          thus from the positive *grasp*
     to the mountain, from mountain to Cloud
        from Cloud to blue depth of sky
            all is *gradation*

[7]

We have traced picture into hieroglyphic
                    and hieroglyphic into arbitrary character—
                    but go further!

        see! how few diversities of character there are
                        impossible except by sense to know
                whether a mark be 'e' or 'i'
                    (or an 'a' or an 'o' or an 'u')
                        or 'n' or 'r' or 'l'
                            or even 'm' or 'u' or 'w'
        eleven letters one mark

                So by increase
                    may not any one thing
                        come to mean all things?

        The foregoing observation a mere sophism

                    What if all were to come together?

            No! all we can deduce is this
        the assimilating Intellect may reduce all forms into any one
                                    representative of all
                but still Intellect demands Distinction

        That form which is now an 'n'
                    may elsewhere be 'a' or 'w'
                            or 'i' or 'r' or 'd'
            but no six characters
                could without diversity
                        convey the word 'inward'

                    N.B. half a page wasted in Nonsense
            and a whole page in confutation
                    But such is the nature of exercise—
                        I walk a mile for health—
                    & then another
                                to return home again

[8]

On a heap of glowing wood embers
        throw Chips and Shavings
they will quietly and moulderingly change
           into the substance of fire—

    but apply even the smallest Match
               the faintest *flame*
      with a thousandfold less Heat
        will set the whole instantly on flame—

Can it be supposed
        the tapering blue flame of a match
            a bit of phosphorus
      more intense
       than a Hearth of glowing Embers?

     some business of affinity
         concerned here

[9]

I had sealed a Letter /
    & wanted the stick of sealing wax, for another Letter /
could not find it—
     searched & searched—
              pockets
                fobs
         impossible places
           literally vanished
and where was it?
    stuck to my *Elbow*
  I having leaned upon it
     ere it had yet grown cold

[10]

Seeing a nice bed of glowing Embers
                    with one Junk of firewood well placed
        like the remains of an old Edifice
                                and another
                                        well nigh mouldered
                                    corresponding
                felt an impulse
                            to put on three pieces
                exactly completed this perishable architecture

tho' it was 11 ° clock
                        tho' I was that instant going to bed
                & in common ideas
                            no possible use in it

                                        Hence I seem
                    (for I write, not having yet gone to bed)
            to suspect
                    this desire of totalizing
                                    of perfecting
        may be bottom-impulse of many actions
                never brought forward
                            as an avowed, or even conscious motive /

thence I proceed   ·
                            to think of restlessness in general
        its *fragmentary* nature
                its connection with the pleasures derived from *Wholeness*

                            & the yearning left behind
                    by those pleasures
                                often experienced

One of Steve Tilden's images
in the translation exchange

CROSSING OVER
WITH A BURDEN
(*ON TRANSLATION*)

Exchanges with Steve Tilden

[1]

In this version
    with each returning life
        the thread is cut

           The fledgling shivers on her perch
              spring sun gilds her downy wing

        Clotho the spinner in her robe of stars
      the heavens revolving on her distaff
                her spindle this spinning earth

     Lachesis pouring oblivion
           from a stoneware pithos
    Atropos wielder of shears

              Older even than Time
           keepers of the archives of heaven
      inventors of the sacred letters
           alpha, beta, eta, tau, upsilon
                rudiments of beauty

Language, a bird call, a beginning

        Atropos in her widow's weeds
                severs the thread
        and the soul is launched
            in a flurry of feathers

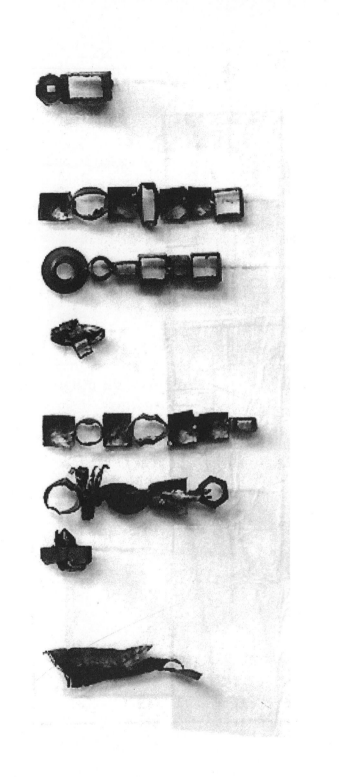

[2]

Its mask laid aside
    the word stands for a moment naked in the tiring-house
        hurries change of costume
            meditates accent, intonation

      The mask a filbert shell
          preserving its kernel
            an ancient tongue

The translator cuts in steel a frozen music
      the words migrate, repeating
        their alphabet
        upbeat, downbeat, w m w m w m

They will cross a border to the moist field
      where their cries are foreign

    A thin skin of ice has stilled the rain-puddle
    in the cold air the geese search for a line south
    they cannot sense

    Baying like hounds that have lost their quarry
    in the crisp air the geese form and reform a skein
    they cannot hold

    Winter is early this year

There is no going back, it seems
    in the old country words spring up like weeds in the pasture

        The returning voyager betrayed
          by a quaint vocabulary
        a halting cadence

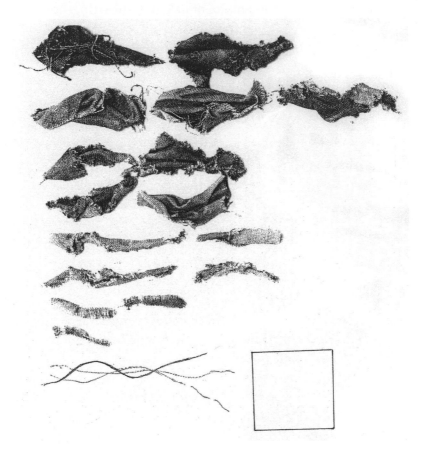

[3]

The mechanics of invasion

> Iron shipped from the Welsh hills
> drawn into lines through prairie grass
> straight to the golden west

> A knife in living skin
> carving a wound not to be closed forever

> Buffalo lift their heads
> keep their distance in front of the work gangs
> riders watch from the bluffs
> as the iron horse shatters the night
> in a shower of sparks and steam

The iron enters their soul

> Opening of territory
> for the better health of the body politic
> the world it cuts
> nothing will stitch together

Hills thick with evergreens
> russet madrones and scrubby oaks
> surrender to logging roads, smallholdings, coastal settlements
> canyons of steel and concrete

> Progress, merely a substitution
> one language for another

[4]

Imagine an island severed from the main
          a new-year's gift to the cartographer's wife
      a fragment sheared from the ghost continent
                   that fading memory

Now imagine this argosy's stately voyage
          this ark, freighted with ferns and dinosaurs
      its unperceived millennial progress
                   journey to landfall

At harbour imagine a chaotic docking
          the great bulk driven into and under Asia
      birthing a mountain range into air
                   like crumpled paper

Imagine an island of monkeys and mango trees
          guarded by a palisade of rocks and glaciers
      preserving a luxuriant kingdom, a Xanadu
                   and beyond it sand

A conversation repeated across aeons
             separation of continents, metamorphosis
      upheaval, erosion, ancient cousins, mountain and plain
                   poetry and prose

          High peaks, the tribesmen call
                   their only friend
         Marshland between two rivers
                 the first paradise

               Every hill and valley
                   its own dialect

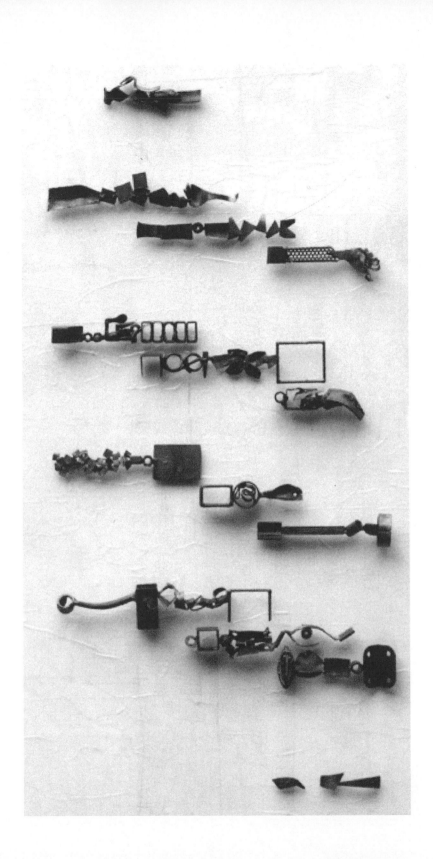

[5]

Language an accumulation of fragments
                        vulnerable to distance and neglect
                Mayan glyphs choked by liana vines
        cartouches of the Ptolemies unread under sand

                        Ideograms of twisted metal
                                hulks on the ocean floor
                                        shrapnel
                                pillars from a ruined skyscraper

Archaeology of interpretation
                crossing a rope bridge jungle to jungle

                Leaves played upon by wind
                        vibrate at every frequency
                                this whispered music
        Notes of an ancient chant
                        they rehearse in autumn air
                                a dying fall
        Scattered on the ground
                        yellow soul-husks
                                their edges barely touch
        The valley heavy with fog, nothing
                        is what it seems, beautiful
                                she says, like a book

A sweet disorder in the dress
                as she disrobes
                        confusion of silks pulled over her head
        flourish of colours resolving themselves into stillness
                this peony blossoming on its slender stem
                do more bewitch me than when art
                        is too precise in every part

[6]

Translatio

Change of ownership
   as of money alienated from its true possessor

     Graft of scion on root stock
    foreign fruit, the tree singing a new tongue

Then translation, trope, figure of speech
  says the grammarian, making use of a trope

     Translatio itself a translation of *metaphora*
     crossing over with a burden
      hauling by wagon

Μεταφορά
  Transfer of attributes
    as of meaning from one word to another

        Into reality
     into another language
    to a regiment in the provinces
       to a new bank account

A verb
 To cast about, the dog on a deer's track doubling for scent

 To change, alter, confound, use a word in a fresh sense

To investigate an etymology, its own for example

    The university men, says Will Kemp
   they smell too much of that writer Ovid
     and that writer Metamorphosis

[7]

Crossing water
　　　enter another country

　　　　　　Charon poles a shipload of skeletons
　　　　　　　　　　　　　one of them playfully
　　　　　　　trails in oblivion a bony hand

A rocking rhythm, almost a cradle song
　　　　　draws to a jetty lost in cypress shade
　　　　　　　among the island's evergreens
　　　　　　　　　hints at stone-hewn habitations
　　　　　　　lit by an uncanny gleam

　　　　　　　　　Isle of the Dead, a shared nightmare
　　　　　this painter from the high country
　　　dreaming the century to come, the age of apocalypse
　　　　　　　and the exiled Russian
　　　　　　haunted by the *Dies Irae*
　　　　　　　　lullaby to hush a Black Death's children

　　Sombre resonances
　　　　　of a continent grown weary

In the new world an image of paint and light
　　　　　the fur traders descend the Missouri as if alive
　　　　　　　study us
　　　　　　so closely in passing, these two
　　　　with their cargo of murder, and the black bear cub
　　　　　　　　in the prow of the canoe

　　They go down the river, steady
　　　　　between their reflections and the luminous sky

　　　　　A moment later they would have been gone

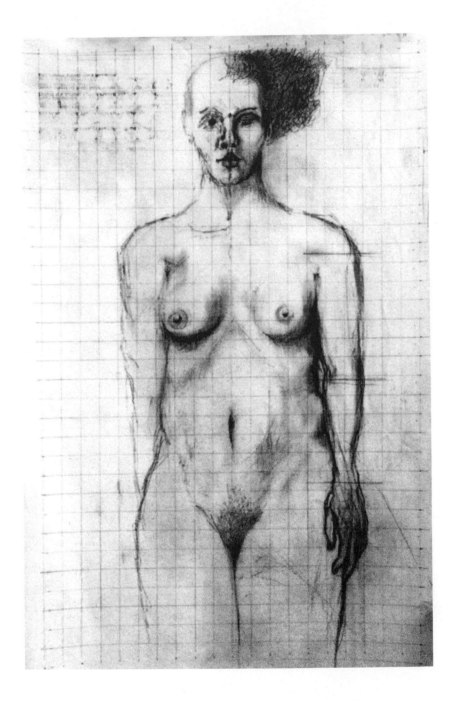

[8]

About 20 years ago
   (he sets the story near the birth of the young republic)
        a party of these Indians (Hietans, or Comanches)
  crossed the River Grand to Chihuahua
     residence of the governor-general of the five internal provinces
lay in ambush and made prisoner the governor's daughter
            a young lady going in her coach to mass

The governor sent my informant a thousand dollars
        for the purpose of recovering his daughter
          he immediately dispatched (says Sibley)
   a confidential trader then in his employ
     with the 1000 dollars in merchandise, who repaired
  to the nation, found her, and purchased her ransom

But to his great surprise she refused to return with him to her father
   and sent by him the following message:

            The Indians had disfigured her face
  tattooing it according to their fancy and ideas of beauty
    a young man of them had taken her for his wife
      by whom she believed herself pregnant
  she had become reconciled to their mode of life
          and was well treated by her husband
  and she should be more unhappy by returning to her father
        than by remaining where she was

Which message was conveyed to her father
    who rewarded the trader by a present of 300 dollars more
  for his trouble and fidelity

    And his daughter is now living with her Indian husband
      by whom she has three children

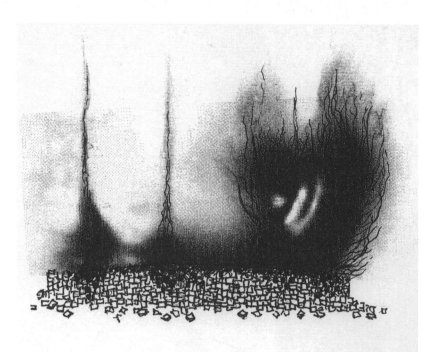

[9]

When the library of Alexandria burned
    words of Aeschylus filled the air
        charred flecks of papyrus

As the brilliance of Calvus dwindled to a scatter of phrases
    poems of his friend Catullus survived the sack of Rome
        in the bung of a wine-cask

Something is recovered
          The shepherd boy by the Dead Sea
      wakening the Essenes asleep in their cave
    A minor proclamation in three scripts
        voicing a million hieroglyphs

Time the great translator
    capriciously selects from a babble of tongues

      Carved figures stretch their empty hands
          we guess at their burden
    In faded cloth
        a marriage quilt holds echoes

      Caged near Pisa
under a hurricane of pain and delusion
    that prisoner reads Confucius

        poetry pouring out of him
          an almost unbearable beauty

      Cut loose, broken
    mapping from the fragments an earthly paradise

[10]

A place of assembly
          temenos: an enclosure, severed by a furrow
     nemeton: a grove, a sacred wood

               wilderness beginning at the city wall
          streets lit by lamplight, darkness beyond

     Three horses stand together
     in the pasture below the farm
     their eyes open to danger

     Where a blood-red half-moon
     touches the ploughed acre
     the stream at the field's edge
     escapes, too small to matter

     Out of a cloud shaped exactly
     like a diving falcon's wing
     the comet begins its swing
     out beyond the galaxy

     The tilted dipper pours
     a hundred million milky stars

     Our round fragmented world
     attempts by their faint light
     to pull the stitches tight
     so the patchwork will hold

The perfect dwelling a square enclosing a courtyard garden
     sanctuary of trees and water
          echo of a cloister, a sequestered court
               the perfect city an interlock of piazzas
                    bounded by porticoes

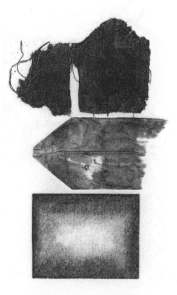

[11]

Memory palace, the mind an attic room
        picture gallery, cabinet of curiosities

                metal fragments joined by the welder's torch
                        bird song, harmony of oak and ash

            Such have I been as you
            are now, and should learn
            to sail with all winds,
            defend all blows, make
            music with all strings,
            know all the ways to
            the wood, and like a
            good travelling hackney
            learn to drink of all waters

            Heywood, a lute tuned to his times

The world so various, our little span
        contains only what it can hold, a banquet of sense

                There is a choice of honey, delicate
                taste of early summer linden, high
                summer buckwheat, or fall treasure,
                dark and thick, gathered by forest bees

                When eating ribs, the nearer the bone
                the sweeter the meat. After lovemaking
                cold applejuice; after a quarrel sweet tea

                Live hard, relax deep, don't jump their
                hurdles. Go as far as you can, then
                that's it. And let your words be few
                and savoury, crisp outside, tender within

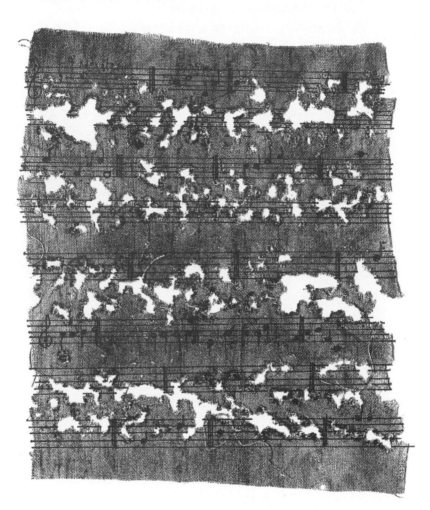

[12]

To house a life this microcosm his symphony
    he felt the cadences fall into place
        out of his experience and a massive hope in the future
    in the struggle to translate complexity
        that march theme came to him

An enigma building his border *Lacrimae*
        stone by stone into a cathedral
           movements toward a *mappa mundi*

The sky one day filled horizon to horizon with fleecy clouds

        Completed the piece
    wrapped myself in a thick overcoat & sat
loathed the world—the house empty and cold—
    shivered & longed to destroy the work of my hands—
all wasted
        that march theme striding

A military bearing
        the moustache a first line of defence
his impeccably knotted tie
        silk handkerchief a flourish in the jacket pocket
        a delight in dogs and kites
golf, hunting and fishing, his gift for friendship

    Once he helped dig a flock of sheep from a snowdrift
        fragments penned

Finding amidst warring breezes an air *Nobilmente e semplice*
    striding across open country
        cutting a long path through the woods

[13]

Inherited essences, fugitive aromas, flash of a blue jay
against thunderclouds, passed down too carelessly

A half century ago leaving Windsor that nest of singing
birds, saw at dusk the hurried assemblages of tree branches,
broken chairs, scavenged house timbers piled into heaps,
some with the ragged-trousered sacrifice enthroned already,
king of the old year, a necessary death. Speeding westwards
into darkness, she saw the first bonfires ignited, ascent
and starburst of stray rockets, then gradually in all directions
round each fire a circle of lit faces, the flames now leaping,
sparks and exhalations, Catherine wheels, Roman candles,
to celebrate old martyrdoms. At last the world of fire
consumed itself, dwindled to glowing embers, cooled.
She crossed the dark estuary, its air heavy with smoke.

Sleeping body, earth smell after rain. Moles and badgers
root in its arteries, and restlessly the dog fox hunts
through thickets, across open fields, testing with his nose
the still remembered secrets. Each memory a dragon
biting his own tail, workings of an abandoned pit.
The sculptor sleeps on his bed of slate. His dreams
are molten bronze poured into the crannies of his skull,
kings and queens like standing stones, spears and helmets
in the cave mouth, relics of bear and hippopotamus,
jawbone and pelvis, rib and shoulder-blade, old texts
deciphered, pottery fragments, days and nights half
forgotten, fins of fossil fish moving in the darkness.

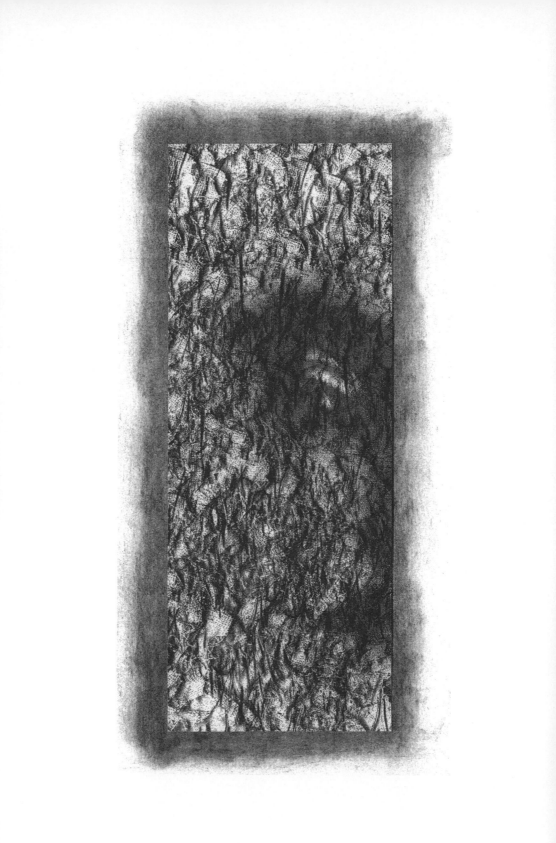

[14]

Parched fields like platters of bronze
                sun focused through a burning glass
                                skins tempered by heat

This was his vision, a wide staircase
and belles in white taffeta, angels
ascending and descending. He stored
the stained water-flask and uniform
and moved to adorn his wooded hill
with temples of peace, white columns,
hint of Athens in the porticoes, the girls'
straight backs, their marble figures.

The general is gone, a ramrod of bone.
His girls, and their children, are ghosts.
In this room at the head of the staircase
they stood in the light of their best years.

Now an ivy curtain fills the tall window
these women talk about the sunlit days
their voices shaded with knowledge. Time
has flowed through them like an underground
river. They are caves they have hardly begun
to explore. They step further into the dark.

And you two, are you still firing moss-green bowls
              in your Han courtyard
                        hedged by bamboo and softened by water
its atrium trailed with vine-tendrils,
                              where the company reclined by candle-light
                                that evening of wine and poetry?

Horace, Odes 1:9

Vides ut alta stet nive candidum
Soracte, nec iam sustineant onus
    silvae laborantes, geluque
        flumina constiterint acuto.

dissolve frigus ligna super foco
large reponens atque benignius
    deprome quadrimum Sabina
        o Thaliarche, merum diota.

permitte divis cetera, qui simul
stravere ventos aequore fervido
    deproeliantis, nec cypressi
        nec veteres agitantur orni.

quid sit futurum cras fuge quaerere et
quem Fors dierum cumque dabit lucro
    appone, nec dulcis amores
        sperne puer neque tu choreas,

donec virenti canities abest
morosa, nunc et campus et areae
    lenesque sub noctem susurri
        composita repetantur hora,

nunc et latentis proditor intimo
gratus puellae risus ab angulo
    pignusque dereptum lacertis
        aut digito male pertinaci.

[15]

From the Sabine Farm

Fresh snow gleaming on Soratte, look—
    branches burdened to breaking,
        streams at an icy standstill.

Throw logs on the fire, let Giorgio pour
    that local wine you've been hiding,
        it must be ready by now.

Life is out of our hands. Storm swells subside,
    gales blow over. Cypresses, rowans
        stop tossing their limbs.

When playing the odds, spend every windfall.
    Giorgio wants to make love to his girl.
        You could go dancing.

Silver hair is snow country. Don't squander
    your youth. Stroll in the piazza,
        make secret rendezvous.

Her soft laugh gives her away in the shadows.
    The bracelet slides down her arm,
        the ring from her finger.

[16]

Two thousand winters scrolled by impatient hands
     thread unbroken at Tu Fu's hermitage
          explorations in the mountains
               laughter and friendship

     A passing encounter on the longest journey
          arrange, he said, the contents of the heap into a line
(the 'l' wittily straying above the measure,
     from Virginia and Leonard's press)
          a poem is true if it hangs together

His rooms that October morning
   stray wisps of talk, memory of Cavafy
     standing absolutely motionless at a slight angle to the universe

          On the wall in golden lamplight
     his Mughal miniatures, amber worry-beads
          flotsam of an itinerant life

Young Alexander asked the Celts what most they feared
     received a jesting answer, that the sky might fall.
Lord of three continents he came to Taxila,
   still burdened with questions:
          Where are your graves?
Which are more numerous, the living or the dead?
     Which is the stronger, life or death?

The brahmans answered lightly
     displaying their wealth
          date palms and running water

          How isolate and proud
     and through what gulfs encountered

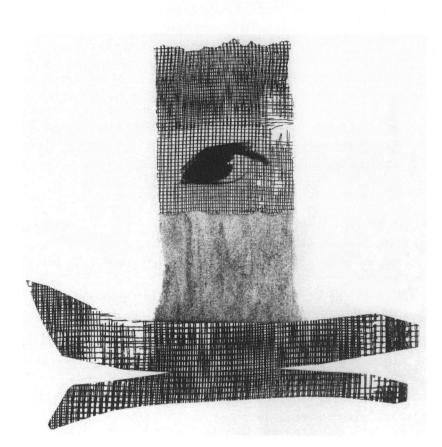

[17]

On all sides water
        and of all islands and peninsulas
      anchored here by chance
                its fourteen brine springs
       two peaks guarding a glacial valley
            vineyards and hay fields
                sweet with clover and lavender
                 translated to honey

An anthology of influences
      even this creamy sheet an inheritance from wasps

      Last on this promontory
          Indian Charlie and his fourth wife
        planned a great potlatch, rowed out at dawn
           trolling for salmon
          the canoe that evening floating empty

The wood abandoned, its only sound
      a woodpecker drumming

          The old ones turned to stone
            reclined at the water's edge

They became seals, herons
      haunting the estuary at dusk
        thumbnail sketches, ink on silver sheen

           To draw is to draw together

John Dee, table from the *Book of Enoch* (1583, printed 1659)

FRAGMENTA EX LIBRIS MYSTERIORUM

John Dee in Poland and Bohemia, 1583-1589

The mathematician John Dee, unofficial magus and astrologer to the Queen, prime consultant for the expeditions to Muscovy and the Northwest Passage, and owner of the finest scientific library in England, first met Gerard Mercator in 1547, when at twenty-one he studied with him at Louvain. Mercator, the leading cartographer of his day, corresponded widely with innovators in many disciplines, among them the historians Camden and Hakluyt, the cartographers Ortelius and Llwyd, Hogenberg the painter, Plantin the publisher, the alchemist emperor Rudolph II, and possibly the anatomist Vesalius, his fellow-student at Louvain.

No correspondence survives between Dee and Mercator after 1577, but they could have been in contact during Dee's last continental journey, and may even have exchanged letters until 1593, when Mercator suffered the paralysis that led to his death the following year. After returning from the continent, Dee toiled in obscurity till the end of his life in 1608 or the first months of 1609.

Dee to Mercator, Mortlake, December 1608

Sunday. The weavers' shuttles silent. I sit
in my warren on Thames bank. Six o'clock
I will cross the road to worship. *The shades
lengthen and evening comes, the busy world
is hushed, the fever of life over and our work
done*. Wherever we have lived, Gerard, it was
under the shadow of a church. Today's snow
has erased every footprint. I am truly alone.

Did our faith protect us? Sixty years are past
since our first meeting. You were a scarecrow
scrawny from months in prison. You told me
five of your cellmates burned, but you escaped
the Grand Inquisitor. What was the charge?
Wishing to speak directly to God, without
priest as intermediary. Your inspiration
was the Family of Love, a harmless dream.

Our Familists Plantin and Ortelius also
felt afraid. Plantin fled for a time to Paris,
a badger harried by terriers. You left
Louvain's hive for undisturbed obscurity
on the banks of Rhine. I always loved
the rituals of mother church, its theatre
of words and music, the natural magic,
bread and wine turning to body and blood.

One may recite both creeds and still be open
to certain mysteries. To write those words
is a death sentence. He who speaks truth
should have one foot in the stirrup, say
the Turks. Your throne, Gerard, is set
beside the river of light, no human hand
can touch you there. I hope before long
to join you. I have outlived my time.

Nothing prepares us (you remember this)
for the sound of a prison door closing,
terror of finality in the rattle of keys,
a foretaste, possibly, of eternal doom.
I lay for two years in that stinking straw,
every day the same array of questions.
Bartlett Green, who rotted there with me,
provided the wrong answers and died.

The story I have concealed for years
will be safe with you today. Its heart
is a puzzle too intricate for solution,
a locked box I am afraid to open.
Let us talk of doubt. You remember
my aphorisms dedicated to you, those
certainties? Their ugly stepchild was
the *Encomium Dubitationis*. Here it is.

In Praise of Uncertainty: Four Aphorisms

In a foreign city, my outlandish tongue
and clothes, my manners clumsy, bed cold,
the dishes salt and sour. I am so young
in experience, and already too ancient
in books. Shipwrecked, drifting, I hear
a voice in my right ear: 'Johannes Dee,
enjoy this strangeness always. It is thee.'

A man clearing fish-scales from his stall
flings from the bucket a rainbow arc
through sunlight at a blood-spattered wall.
The droplets shimmer round his head.
He stands suspended in his own glory
at the end of a rain-glazed cobbled street
where he treads water with hobnailed feet.

Fashion a hollow sphere of copper or tin
with a like cylinder of the same diameter
and equal height. Now you can imagine
their relationship. Pour water out of one
into the other. The ratio is two to three.
Yet human to human, instant by instant
the balance of attraction is inconstant.

The bells chimed midnight. Under the tower
forgotten by the sleeping town, I embraced
your shoulders, we savoured a last hour.
Releasing one another then, we drew
a thread like wire, unseen, not to be broken.
Fragrance of roses in air, a clouded moon
obeyed nature's law: *More hid than shown.*

Travel Notes, September 1583

Lord Albert Laski meeting me on water in dead
of night wherries to Gravesend a great tilt-boat
from Gravesend to our ships by sunrise a double
fly-boat of Denmark another a boyer a pretty ship
with little wind hoisted sail and began our voyage
in great danger of perishing on the spit midnight
cutting our cable committing to the hands of God
wind served to recover Queenborough back again

Monday we made to land in small fisher-boats
sailyard and sail entangled on the fly-boat the top
being fast above the wind and stream carrying
off below of necessity the boat must sink but
God in his providence had greater care of us
so we became clear the boat half full the billow
of the seas still beating in, one of our boatmen
lost his long oar out of the boat into the water

E.K. with a great gauntlet did empty most part of
the water else must needs have sunk by all reason
at length up crooked creek the master standing
with his boots would have taken me out in arms
fell with me where I was foul arrayed in water
and ooze. God be praised for ever, danger ended
with so small grief Thursday all night at anchor
so by land's end into main sea to the north-east

Saturday we fell on Holland none of our mariners
master nor pilot knew the coast therefore to main
sea again with great fear and danger wind so scarce
Sunday we came to Brielle to an anchor lay in ship
all night Thursday Rotterdam in a hoy of Amsterdam
Friday came to Gouda lay within town in the ship
Saturday Haarlem to Amsterdam by contrary wind
went within land in little scouts to Leeuwarden.

A Kind of Noah's Ark

Lord Laski, Myrcopskie his man, Jane with
our brace of boys Arthur and baby Rowland
two-year old Katharin my servants Mary
Elizabeth John Crocker and nurse, Edward
Kelley and his Joan, two horses a hundred
alchemical manuscripts six hundred books
like to have drowned, the table of practice
God's providence and mercy over all amen.

The Language of Adam, Cracow

For lo the time is come the kings of the earth
will become mad and I will build my temple
in the woods even in the desert places become
a serpent in the wilderness in 49 voices or
callings the natural keys 48 (one not to be
opened) gates of understanding all things
contained within the compass of nature
cease now with me for no more descendeth

E.K. immediately fell into a new doubting
the verity of these actions our instructors
all devils he would no more receive A B C
John your boy can well enough deliver you
these letters you need not me &c. I referred
all to God so do I not doubt but God will
according to his accustomed goodness provide
that is best for my vocation here on earth &c.

I had some understanding of these holy words
intending thereby to have induced E . K . to like
better the manner of our friends' proceeding
unless of this strange language letter by letter
we might for want of true pronunciation miss
the effect expected again he said our teachers
were deluders he could two years have learned
the seven liberal sciences so he went from me

Wednesday Gabriel and Nalvage appeared
after manifold prayers the frame of the stone
gave a crickling no hand touching it to E.K.
it seemed the sound of a bunch of keys shaken
Gabriel said these keys we deliver are mysteries
all things moving and moved within the world
in this the life of MOTION, in whom all tongues
are moved as plain here as in their nakedness

DAIOI of him that liveth for ever RIZ I am PAL
for PLERV a strong seething MZAZO make me DO
and OZLACIM in power NARMAZ show yourselves
DOQONC unto his servants AC therefore RACAZ
move LEHOG saith the first UZROT Arise NODIAI
of the all-powerful NINAM in the mind QO but
EGAT as is not SROC such FORT a building NAON
you are become PAL for NOGNOZO manifold winds

A great storm or temptation to E.K. of doubting
misliking our instructors and their doings and of
contemning any thing I could do I bare all things
for God his sake at length the curtain was opened
spoke Gabriel the time shall come the oak beaten
with every storm shall be a table in the prince's
hall. E.K.: There appeareth a great globe turning
upon two axle-trees he showeth the North Pole

From heaven a mist covereth a great place a park
enclosed with fire four rivers out of it in the gate
stand three men one in a long gown with pleats
the other in a cassock the third in the rough skin
of a beast is this the Paradise Adam was banished
out of? Δ: It should seem this must be on the earth
Nalvage: It is. Δ: To what part is Atlantis? Nalvage:
Prepare for tomorrow's action. Δ: Most gladly

Thursday E.K. came not I went to his study door
he gave me a short and resolute answer he would
never more have to do with these actions so I went
into my study again committed the cause to God
after half an hour or less he came speedily out
brought in his hand Cornelius Agrippa his works
in one chapter provinces out of Ptolemaeus, he
inferred our spiritual instructors were coseners

I replied very glad you have a book wherein
these names are expressed but for all this E.K.
remained of his evil intent and I committed God
his cause into his own care, as may be best so
be it Thursday Friday Saturday lost by E.K.
his disquietness God be merciful unto us
Monday I said the Lord's Prayer after this
my wife her speeches and usage toward E.K.

Friday he plainly and at large made manifest
his conversion to God from the practices with
wicked spirits moreover about nine or ten days
he did intend to have gotten away secretly
thanks to the Almighty for his power showed
in the conversion of E.K. Wednesday early
lying in his bed awake one patted him on the head
gently clothed with feathers wreathed all over

There appeared to him four castles every gate
one trumpeter and after them an infinite number
Spirit: I expound the vision the four houses are
the angels of the earth hereby you may subvert
whole countries without armies know treasures
of the waters and unknown caves of the earth
a doctrine for you only instrument of the world
E.K.: The will of God be done. Δ: Amen.

On Friday E.K. great temptations not to credit
this action said unto by a voice, our instructors
use cavillation of our disordered life through him
must the words be heard none spoke directly to me
I made a short discourse to God of my just dealing
hitherto of the Book of Enoch after this appeared
a man all black naked: When thou art at the end
of thy journey it shall be told. Δ: Hallelujah. Amen.

In Wawel Castle

At audience with the Polonian king
my Lord Laski only being by thrust
my hand into the stone lion's mouth:

Who nurtured you from the cradle?
Is it not that King of Glory? Did he not
raise you with his powerful arm, from
an ordinary soldier to a greater one
and so to the greatest kingdom? Why
did you introduce such a dark cloud
of fog and ingratitude between God
and your soul? Your sins are numbered
and multiplied in heaven abandon
your impiety I will set aside my anger
and your remaining days will be
confirmed in fortitude governors
of the world will fall before your feet
and your sword be terror of nations.

This month the king drew up his will
we returned to Prague unsatisfied.

The Charm

The first day of August our journey
toward Prague we came in eight days
began in the excellent little stove or study
of Dr Hajek his house by Bethlehem
on the green mound the house inherited
from his alchemist father Simon Bakalar
hieroglyphical birds, fishes, flowers, fruit
on the south side uppermost written:

Immortale decus par gloriaque illa debentur
cuius ab ingenio est discolor hic paries.
Everliving fame and glory are due
to him whose thoughts this wall imbue.
Candida si rubeo mulier nupta when
lilywhite woman marries russet man
creating in conjunction one from two
Sun and Moon giving birth to Stone,

Sol adit Lunam per medium Sun enters
Moon becoming one and spreads his sail
transit per ecliptica navigates the heavens
chasing the Moon on her declining path
no moonlight save by Sun she would remain
by her companion her dead husk illumined.
Si Rebus scires quid esset tu reperires
rummage the Arcana, find what you seek.

Haec ars est cara Sweet this art and fleeting
and of rare device, all adepts should know
the elixir's fruit may not be plucked
but by initiation to the essential stone
etsi aliam viam quaerit he who seeks
a separate path will never find the way
rust is the means, earth become moist
reveals its golden heart and so an end.

The Hasid's Apprentice

Ghosts are commonplace. I have seen trees
melt into armed men, moonlight gleam
on breastplate suddenly resolved again
back to darkness. Soft feet have hurried
past me where I was alone, and once, no
person being by, a voice close by my ear
whispering urgently 'Prsh, prsh, prsh'.

In younger days, they say, the Rabbi Loewe
fashioned from clay a servant, breathed
life into his nostrils, placed on his brow
the sacred name. This servant, the golem,
inhabited the attic above the synagogue
descending the outside wall like a spider
when the rabbi had need of his strength.

One sabbath the community at prayer
the golem left alone, purposeless,
clambered to the street, strode roaring
into the market, overturned fruit stalls
snatched up fistfuls of sausage and fish
drove a butcher to his knees with one
blow, in the confusion a cry went up

'Murder! Murder!' and the rabbi
rushed from the synagogue, tore
the name from the creature's brow
and the golem crumbled to dust.
I have seen him many times, the rabbi
walking the streets pensive, a creator
mourning his fallen masterpiece.

The Emperor Rudolf

In the palace antechamber beheld
the pleas of countless petitioners
scratched in the plaster. One hour
sufficed to house them in rooms
of a memory palace, as we learned
you and I in separate captivities.
Survivors owe the dead at least
a true accounting of their names.

In the mean space the Chamberlin
led me by the skirt of the gown
where the Emperor sat at a table
looking back whether any man
were in the chamber we were alone
I began to declare my lifetime spent
with pain to come by best knowledge
it pleased God to send me his light

His holy angel two years and a half
used to inform me no man could wish
so much I am now before your Majesty
and have a message the Angel of the Lord
rebuketh you for your sins believe me
you shall triumph if you will not hear
the Lord his foot against your breast
will throw you headlong from your seat

The Emperor said he did believe me
would henceforth take me to his care
and some such words (of favour
promised) I heard not well he spoke
so low. I took my leave of him and so
came through the Ritter Stove or guard-
chamber and down and home. I had
a large hour audience of his Majesty.

On Truth and Forgetting

I dreamed a letter in one of the alphabets
so obscure its first significance was lost.
Some thought it was used to season words
of grief, as salt water lifts a funeral barge.
Others believed in the old days it guarded
that handful of expressions that told the truth.

What do we have to light the way but our own
lantern? The others cannot help. They know
their torches barely light the room's corners
or even the well of shadow two steps ahead.

Codes

Banished from court my household adrift in Saxony
Frankfurt a round of goldsmiths and money-lenders
then crossing the Hyrcanian forests into Silesia,
Breslau city of a hundred bridges a brief haven,
lodged on Sand Island in the cathedral's shadow
in our declining fortunes supported by your friends
Monau the cartographer and the astronomer Dudith.

A patron is a magnet. We were iron filings, drawn
from city to city. How clever you were, Gerard,
to find your mouse-hole. I remember attic rooms
and the angel voices speaking only to E.K. their
(do I acknowledge this?) incomprehensible texts.
Mean time I sent the Privy Council dispatches
cloaked in my own impenetrable letter code.

At Breslau I heard from my informant in Prague
this story current there. A woman seeking E.K.
called to him in his house under the castle wall.
He leaned from a window hatless, and she saw
he had no ears. In rage he enchanted her baby
with a donkey's head. The pious lady prayed
to the Virgin Mary and so restored her child.

Thus in our time we are subjects for fairy tales.

Travel Notes, September 1586

Wagons mired in fall mud
pigs grubbing under oak trees.
A lake, a church on its far shore
its spire a tall bodkin. That man
kneeling on his roof hammering
into place a lath. E.K. angered
with his wife, then reconciled.
A fiery sunset, air washed clean
hot coals in a furnace streaked
with steely blue, the river aflame.
Boys fishing, joined by threads
to the blaze. The castle doors
thrown open, cobbled yard
and safe at last. In the park three
peacocks stalked in the dusk
bronze leaves and polished
acorns thick on the ground.

The Cross-Matching

Under Rozemberg protection
Kelley turned alchemist
all the angels less attentive
the fishponds locked in ice.

With spring a visitation from
Michael archangel, we must
share our wives in common.
The women incredulous, E.K.
adamant I called the archangel
to be clear he confirmed they
must be shared. So a single
sentence confounds a world.

No more on this. I crossed
a continent and sixty years
to find a smooth pomaded
courtier become a charlatan.
I had created a golem, but
where was the sacred name?

Travel Notes, March 1589

Rode out into frozen air
our baby one year old, sun
crimson over the fishpond

White mist on the lake, ancient
oak trees marked our departure
iron gates closing behind us

A Last Salutation

Taste of wormwood, remembrance of Laski
who in that earlier shuffle bid fair to be King
of Poland. We viewed the eclipse together
in my dark chamber, where lenses (simple
magic) draw the world into my inner study
through a pinhole. Laski called it *antrum
Platonis*. We saw a wherryman on Thames
and a gardener grafting trees across the river.

I understand a genius in Delft uses this device
to assist his painting in oils. When the eclipse
was near, I set a leaf to catch the image. What
satisfaction, as moon traverses sun, to prove
our calculations. Nature answers to prophecy.
As the room became entirely dark I was given
a vision of you at your window. We observed
the phenomenon from our several angles.

I remembered your voice across half a century
speaking gently to a student: 'An eclipse is but
a momentary obstruction of the light. Failure
in curiosity is permanent.' We were granted
places in paradise garden, a chance to taste
the fruit of knowledge, and were banished
by the stern archangel. The bell is calling
faithful to evensong. Can you hear it, Gerard?

Your ever-curious pupil—

Δ.

Η ΛΑΜΠΑ ΤΟΥ ΚΑΤΑ ΤΟ ΛΥΚΑΥΓΕΣ

Καλησπέρα, λοιπόν· οἱ δυό τους πάλι, ἐνώπιος ἐνωπίῳ,
ἡ λάμπα του κι αὐτός,—τὴν ἀγαπάει, κι ἂς φαίνεται
ἀδιάφορος κι αὐτάρεσκος· κι ὄχι μονάχα
γιατὶ τὸν ἐξυπηρετεῖ, μὰ πιότερο, καὶ ἰδίως,
γιατὶ ἀξιώνει τὶς φροντίδες του·—λεπτὴ ἐπιδίωση
ἀρχαίων ἑλληνικῶν λυχνιῶν, μαζεύει γύρω της
μνῆμες κ' εὐαίσθητα ἔντομα τῆς νύχτας, ἀπαλείφει
ρυτίδες τῶν γερόντων, μεγεθύνει τὰ μέτωπα,
μεγαλύνει τὶς σκιὲς ἐφηβικῶν σωμάτων, ἐπιστρώνει
μ' ἕνα μειλίχιο φέγγος τὴ λευκότητα κενῶν σελίδων
ἢ τὸ κρυμμένο πορφυρὸ τῶν ποιημάτων· κι ὅταν,
κατὰ τὸ λυκαυγές, τὸ φῶς της ὠχριάζει καὶ ταυτίζεται
μὲ τὸ τριανταφυλλὶ τῆς μέρας, μὲ τοὺς πρώτους θορύβους
ἀπ' τὰ ρουλὰ τῶν μαγαζιῶν, τὰ χειραμάξια, τοὺς ὀπωροπῶλες,
εἶναι μιὰ εἰκόνα ἀπτὴ τῆς ἴδιας του ἀγρυπνίας, κι ἀκόμη
μιὰ γυάλινη γέφυρα ποὺ πάει ἀπ' τὰ γυαλιά του ~~μπροστά κι ἀπ' τῆς~~
~~λάμπας~~
~~κι ἀπ' τὰ γυαλιὰ τοῦ παραθύρου, ὡς ἔξω, ὡς πέρα, καὶ~~
~~πιὸ πέρα~~
~~γυάλινη γέφυρα ποὺ τὸν κρατεῖ πάνω ἀπ' τὴν πολιτεία, μὲς~~
~~στὴν πολιτεία,~~
~~ἐνώνοντας, μὲ τὴ δική του τώρα βούληση, τὴ νύχτα καὶ τὴ μέρα·~~

ὡς τὸ γυαλὶ τῆς λάμπας, κι ἀπ' τὰ γυαλιὰ τοῦ
~~παραθύρου~~, ὡς ἔξω, ὡς πέρα, καὶ πιὸ πέρα—
γυάλινη γέφυρα πὲς τὸν κρατεῖ πάνω ἀπ' τὴν πολιτεία,
μέσα στὴν πολιτεία, ἀξεδίωτα κι ἐνώνοντας,
μὲ τὴ δική τη τώρα θέληση, τὴ νύχτα καὶ τὴ μέρα.

— 11 —

Corrections to the original text given to the author by
Yannis Ritsos. The last of the autograph lines changes
βούληση to θέληση. Ritsos returned to the original word
for 'will/wish' in the second Greek edition. The English
version, 'His Lamp at Dawn', is on page 239.

ALONE WITH HIS WORK

From the modern Greek of Yannis Ritsos

TWELVE POEMS FOR CAVAFY

(Athens, Autumn 1963)

The Poet's Place

The black, carved desk, the two silver candlesticks,
his red pipe. He sits, almost invisible, in the armchair,
keeping the window always at his back. From behind
his spectacles (huge, circumspect) he observes his guest
bathed in light, himself hidden among his words,
in history, behind his masks, distanced, invulnerable,
capturing others' attention with the subtle glints
of a sapphire worn on his finger, the whole time eagerly
savouring their expressions, the moment foolish boys
moisten their lips with their tongues, amazed. And he,
crafty, voracious, sensual, the supreme innocent,
between Yes and No, desire and repentance,
like the scales in God's hand, utterly balanced,
while the light from the window behind his head
sets on him a crown of pardon and sanctity.
'If poetry is not absolution,' he whispered to himself,
'we cannot hope for mercy anywhere.'

His Lamp

The lamp is mild, easy-going; he prefers it
to other kinds of light. Its flame is adjusted
according to the needs of the moment, according
to his eternal, unacknowledged desire. Most of all,
the smell of the oil, a subtle presence
so distinctive at night, when he comes home alone,
such fatigue in his limbs, such frustration
in the weave of his jacket, the seams of his pocket,
every movement seems excessive and intolerable—
the lamp, keeping him occupied—the wick,
the match, the dangerous flame (with its shadows
on the bed, the desk, the walls) and most of all
the glass chimney itself, its frail transparency,
its simple human gesture, right from the start,
compels you: be careful of it, or take care of it.

His Lamp at Dawn

Good evening, then; the two again, face to face,
his lamp, himself—he loves it, even when it seems
indifferent and complacent; and not only
because it works for him, but more, and especially,
because it calls for his attention—a subtle incarnation
of ancient Greek lamps, it gathers to itself
memories and sensitive night insects, erases
old men's wrinkles, broadens their brows,
lengthens the shadows of the boys' bodies, spreads
a mild light on the white of empty pages,
on the secret purple of poems; and when,
at dawn, its light pales and becomes one
with daylight's rose, with the first clatter
of the shop-blinds, handcarts, fruit-stands,
it is a tangible image of his insomnia, and still
a glass bridge leading from his spectacles
to the glass of the lamp, and on to the glass
of the window, and so out, further and further—
a glass bridge carrying him over the city,
through the city, his Alexandria, joining,
as he himself now wills it, night with day.

Putting Out the Lamp

Enormous weariness. Dawn dazzling, treacherous—
marking the end of another of his nights, outdoing
the mirror's polished regret, resentfully chiselling
grooves around his lips and eyes. Useless now,
the lamp's courtesy or the closed curtains. Ineluctable
awareness of the end, the warm breath of a summer night
cooling on the sheets, a few ringlets the only remnants
of a young man's curls—a broken chain—
that same chain—who'd forged that? No use now
for memory or for poems. And yet, that last
moment before sleep, leaning over the lamp's chimney,
to blow on the flame, so it too can go out, he realizes
he is breathing straight into eternity's glass ear an immortal
word, entirely his own, his breath, the primeval sigh.
How the lamp's smoke perfumes his room in the dawn.

His Spectacles

Always between his eyes and their objectives are found
his hermetic spectacles, attentive, absent-minded,
authoritative, eclectic—a faceless glass fortress,
dam, and observatory—a pair of moats
encircling his secret denuded gaze, or rather
the pans of a balance standing—amazingly—not flat
but upright. More than that, an upright balance
that could work beyond emptiness, beyond the
knowledge of emptiness, naked, crystalline, brilliant,
and reflecting on its polished surface a parade
of images inside and outside, a balanced unity
so real, so imperishable, it refuted emptiness entirely.

Hiding Places

'Speech'—he says—'does not mean saying something,
but just that you are speaking. For you to speak
means you will reveal something—how can you speak?'
And then his silence became so translucent
he hid himself completely behind the curtain,
making as if to look out of the window.
But when our eyes on his back irritated him
he turned, peering out through the curtain
as if he were dressed in a long white tunic,
wittily somehow, at odds somehow with the present,
wanting it so (or preferring it), thinking perhaps
this way, by some means, he might divert
our suspicion, our hostility, our unhappiness,
or possibly create some pretext for (he has seen
it coming) our future admiration.

Concerning Form

He said, 'Form is not invented or imposed;
it is contained in things and shows occasionally
in its movement outwards.' Vague platitudes,
we said—what will you show us next? He spoke no more.
He clasped his chin between both hands like a word
in quotation marks. His cigarette remained ambiguous
between his closed lips—a white and glowing mark
of his omissions, everything passed over deliberately
(or perhaps unconsciously?) leaving unsaid his silence.

In the same vague posture, we imagined, sleepless
at a small railway station, under the roof's overhang,
a momentary encounter, one winter night, two
lonely travellers, the taste of coal-dust in their mouths,
from their unfinished journey, from the timeless exchange
of their secret, age-old love. The train's smoke
hung calmly over the two horizontal cones
of the floodlights, solid and sculptural, between the
two departures. He stubbed out his cigarette and left.

Misunderstandings

His ambiguities: infuriating; they cause us suffering,
and he suffers too, manifestly betrayed
by his obscurity, his hesitations, ignorance, cowardice,
his lack of solid principles. Surely he'll entangle us
in his own perplexities. He gazed somewhere beyond us
generously, indulgent somehow (like those needing indulgence)
in his snow-white shirt, impeccable slate-grey suit
with the chrysanthemum in its buttonhole. Still,
when he left, where he'd been standing we saw on the floor
a little bright red pool, beautifully drawn
almost like a map of Greece, a miniature chart
somewhat abstracted, the borders inaccurately drawn,
the frontiers almost lost in the uniform colouring—
a chart in a closed white school in mid-July
the students all gone on a blinding trip to the beach.

Dusk

You know that moment of summer dusk
in the closed room; the faintest rosy gleam
crossing the ceiling beams; the poem
half finished on the table—two verses in all,
unfulfilled promise of a superb journey,
of a kind of freedom, a kind of independence
a kind of (relative, of course) immortality.

Already on the road outside, night's invocation,
the featherlight shadows of gods, men, bicycles,
day shift ended on the building sites, the young
labourers with their tools, their damp, luxuriant hair,
small flecks of lime on their worn overalls,
blend with the evening mist and turn to gods.

Eight stern strokes of the clock on the stairs,
the whole length of the corridor—pitiless strokes
of a ruthless hammer hidden behind the shadowy
glass; and just then the age-old clatter
of those keys, he was never absolutely sure
if they were unlocking or locking up.

Last Hour

There was a perfume left in his room, perhaps only
a memory, and it could have been from the window
half open to the spring evening. He picked out
the things he'd be taking with him. He covered
the big mirror with a sheet. He still felt
in his fingers the touch of well-proportioned limbs
and the touch, the lonely touch, of his pen—no different:
the supreme connection of poetry. He'd never wanted
to deceive anyone. The end was near. He asked
once again: 'Gratitude, perhaps, or the desire
for gratitude?' His ancient slippers had wandered
under his bed. He had no wish to hide them—
(oh certainly, some other time). Only
when he had put the key in his waistcoat pocket,
he sat on his case in the middle of the room
all alone, and began to weep, recognizing
for the first time so piercingly, his innocence.

After Death

Many claimed him, squabbled over him,
perhaps even begged for his suit—that eccentric suit—
formal, impressive, with a certain charm nonetheless,
a certain aura, like that fantastic garb gods wear
when visiting mortals—disguised, they speak
about everyday things in everyday accents, but suddenly
a fold of their garments fills with a breath
of infinity, or of the beyond, as they say.

So they squabbled. What was he to do? They ripped
his clothes, underclothes, they tore even his belt. What was left
was an everyday, naked mortal in a shrinking attitude. Everyone
abandoned him. And just there he turned to marble.
Years later, just there they discovered a radiant statue—
naked, arrogant, tall, carved in Pentelic marble,
the Ageless Ephebe, Tortured by Guilt—that's the name
they gave it; they draped it in a long sack and prepared
a special ceremony for the public unveiling.

Re-Evaluation

The one who died was truly remarkable,
unique; he left us a supreme standard
to measure ourselves, and especially to measure
our surroundings—one man this size,
quite short, another thin, the third
tall as a pair of stilts: no one
with any worth. Nothing, no nothing.
Only we who make proper use
of that standard—but which standard do you mean?—
that is Nemesis, the Archangel's Sword,
have it already sharpened. Now we can
line up everyone and cut off their heads.

SEVEN POEMS FROM *Testimonies I*, ATHENS 1963

The Spider

Sometimes, a chance and altogether insignificant word
lends an unexpected meaning to the poem,
as for example in the abandoned basement, where
no one has been for a while, the large, empty jar—
on its shaded rim pointlessly a spider is walking
(pointlessly for you, but perhaps not for her).

The Same Coolness?

So many days, so many nights so many years—he was tired.
Why such hard work? After midnight, every summer
he would hear groups of young people under his window
laughing, singing, joking. What about him?

As soon as he lit the lamp again for his work
he saw a snail slowly climbing the inkwell. Just as
outside—he remembered—by the well, in the flowerbeds,
on summer evenings, in all the watered gardens,
among the flowers a troop of snails was strolling.

Grey and White

The cafe was empty that afternoon. He sat down alone
to wait, exactly behind the glass of water, with a sense
of empty chairs and darkening windows,
of small sounds stopping at the bottom step
without going in—an expectation so vague,
this fixed, pointless, perverse waiting. In front of him,
above the trees in the park, rose an enormous moon,
deep, dark, behind the glass, itself glass-like,
casting an inky stain on the forehead of the woman
who had sat without a word in the chair next to him.
He raised his glass. The water was warm. The moon warm.
He had to empty both. The woman's hand pure white.

Carnival

The moon's windows lit from inside, lightly steamed over,
the shadow of a hand outlined on them. The hand quietly
opened the window, showed to the wrist, and threw down
a white cotton pierrot costume. For a moment the bells
tinkled on the pavement. He was startled. He looked round.
No one. Streetlamps, telegraph poles, still. Hurriedly he
threw the silver cloak over his shoulders and entered the room,
confident now, smiling, erect, they all applauded him.
Only the bells tinkling just earlier, outside his body,
before his disguise, still rang guiltily in the street,
guiltily and treacherously at once. But soon he realized
only he could hear them amid all the music, lights, and masks.

Alone with His Work

All night he galloped alone, scared, pitilessly spurring
his horse's flanks. They were surely expecting him, he said,
there was great urgency. When he arrived at dawn
no one was waiting. There was no one. He looked everywhere.
Deserted houses, bolted shut. They were asleep.
He could hear his horse panting alongside him—foam
on his mouth, sores on his ribs, and his back flayed.
He hugged his horse's neck and began to weep.
The horse's eyes, large, dark, close to death, were two
solitary watchtowers, far off, where it was raining.

Grades of Perception

The sun sank rosy, orange. The sea
a deep blue-green. In the distance, a boat—
a black, bobbing speck. Someone
got up and called out, 'A boat, a boat.'
The others in the cafe left their chairs, looked.
Indeed, it was a boat. But the one who'd called out,
as if guilty now under the others' fierce looks,
hung his head and murmured, 'I lied to you.'

Ancient Theatre

When at noon he found himself in the middle of the ancient
theatre, this young Greek, unsuspecting, as handsome
as they had been, he gave a shout (not of wonder; he felt
no sense of wonder, and if he had felt it, he
would certainly not have shown it) a simple shout
perhaps from the indomitable joy of youth
or else to test the acoustics of the place. On the other side,
high on the sheer mountain, the echo answered—
the Greek echo that neither imitates nor repeats,
but simply continues at an incalculable pitch
the timeless war-cry of the dithyramb.

Performances

One metre above their chairs, he drew
the red curtain. Before their eyes he performed
their own terrors. Totally nude, he appeared
behind the glass partition, with the nude woman,
and gleams flashed from the five knives.
The clay statue fell in a corner of the bath.
In a sea-green light he drew in the great net
with its hideous, hairy sea-monster. He climbed the centre stair
holding the candlestick. He shouted in the tunnel.
Of course he also broke a plate. The others,
their fears assuaged, applauded and left. He
gathered the fragments of the plate, and all night
tried to fit them back together. Now he had nowhere
to put the food for his dinner. Nor was he hungry.

The Seven

They drew lots from the helmet; took their places
directed almost by fate. When night fell,
not one of the seven was there. A veiled woman
came alone and sat down on the rocks
between a pitcher of wine and a pitcher of oil.

Evening

The olive-trees on the hill, the whitewashed sheepfold,
the gates, the windows, the bath-house, the terraces,
lower down, the beehive tombs—everything so quiet,
like a continuation or a repetition. The guard
went by slowly. The shotgun idle on his shoulder.
On his face, still young, the sunset
sympathetic, peaceful, blood-red. His shadow
huge on the plain like dead Agamemnon.

Obscure Details

When Eumaeus, the swineherd, got up to welcome
the stranger the sheepdogs had announced,
there fell from his knees the beautiful, finely-worked
oxhide he was getting ready for sandals. Later,
as they went to slaughter the two pigs for the feast,
the old man's hospitality, he tightened his belt.
These—the hide, the sandals, the tightening of the belt—
their secret meaning (beyond gods and myths,
beyond symbols and concepts) only poets understand.

THREE POEMS FROM *Stones,* LEROS CONCENTRATION CAMP 1968

Postponements

Days go by. The boat's sail flaps,
the rope frays through. We didn't water the trees.
Last year they withered—no fruit or leaf.
Our women grew old quickly. Little snails
climbed up the walls. When we went down one day,
finally, to clear out the well—nothing:
echoing coolness and a pile of rusty buckets.
We threw them in one by one. The well was dry.

Solution

Forms dissolving, rippling—all kinds of restlessness
and insidious instability—you can hear the sound of water
all round you, changeable, deep, unfathomable. You too,
unfathomable, free almost.
                              In a while poor women came
and some old men, carrying pitchers, cans, saucepans,
fetching water for use at home. The water took new forms.
The river fell silent as if emptied out. Night fell. Doors closed.
Only one woman, without a pitcher, stayed outside, in the garden,
transparent, liquid in the moonlight, with a flower in her hair.

Night

Tall eucalyptus with a broad moon.
A star shimmering in the water.
The sky white, silvery-white.
Pebbles, flayed pebbles all the way up.
The sound nearby in the shallows
of a second, a third fish leaping. The great
astonishing bereavement—freedom.

FROM *Porter's Lodge*, ATHENS 1971

Respectful Comparison

Near here the café, the pharmacy, the cake-shop.
Just beyond them the small florist's. People in a hurry.
Women window-shopping before dusk. Behind
the half-built wall, in the vacant lot with the hollyhocks,
people throw their stuff away—paper plates,
bottles of pills, broken cups, water glasses,
dead flowers.   Old women and dogs meet up here,
scavenge the dump warily, distracted—they miss
the golden sunset. Scavenging like poets for a poem,
these bitter, abandoned women are so thrilled
with a dried orange-peel, a mirror fragment,
a blue tube from the pharmacy still showing
the pale track of a homeless snail across it,
and in its hollow the sound of the northbound train.

FROM *The Far-Off*, ATHENS 1975

Red-Handed

Shine the searchlight full in his face. That way,
hidden in the darkness he'll stand out brightly.
His teeth are fine; he knows that. He's smiling
with the thin moon over the bombed hillside
with the forester's children down by the river.

Burial Ground

1

In honey sun, ghosts
pause. At that moment
the sun grows drowsy

(Here in the potters' quarter
scatter of shards and broken bones)

Presence of unseen
figures, and on the skyline
the virgin Parthenon

2

Midnight under a full moon
Proxeno, pale Amaryllis
Eleni, Phryne and Sophoula
lovely tenantless bodies

In the shadows Chromis
leaning on his spear, Agathon
slightly tipsy, Lysimachus
among the orange flag irises

Memory of silver flesh, and
petals about to fall

LAMENT FOR

THE BABYLONIAN DEAD

Aeschylus, *Persae*, lines 852-1003

Aeschylus fought in the battle of Marathon. Eighteen years later, in 472, he dramatized in *Persians* the naval engagement at Salamis, which ended the Persian invasion. The play sees the events from the viewpoint of the defeated enemy.

Χο. ὦ πόποι ἦ μεγάλας ἀγαθᾶς τε πολ-
     ισσονόμου βιοτᾶς ἐπεκύρσαμεν,
        εὖθ᾽ ὁ γηραιὸς
     πανταρκὴς ἀκάκας ἄμαχος βασιλεὺς
        ἰσόθεος Δαρ-
     εῖος ἄρχε χώρας.

     πρῶτα μὲν εὐδοκίμους στρατιὰς ἀπεφ-
     αινόμεθ᾽, ἠδὲ νομίσματα πύργινα
        πάντ᾽ ἐπεύθυνον.
     νόστοι δ᾽ ἐκ πολέμων ἀπόνους ἀπαθεῖς
        <ἄνδρας> ἐς εὖ πράσσ-
     οντας ἆγον οἴκους.

     ὅσσας δ᾽ εἷλε πόλεις πόρον οὐ διαβὰς Ἅλυος ποταμοῖο,
     οὐδ᾽ ἀφ᾽ ἑστίας συθείς,
     οἷαι Στρυμονίου πελάγους Ἀχελωίδες εἰσὶ πάροικοι
     Θρηίκων <τ᾽> ἐπαύλων,
     λίμνας τ᾽ ἔκτοθεν αἱ κατὰ χέρσον ἐληλαμέναι πέρι πύργον

     τοῦδ᾽ ἄνακτος ἄιον,
     Ἕλλας τ᾽ ἀμφὶ πόρον πλατὺν εὐχόμεναι, μυχία τε Προποντίς,
     καὶ στόμωμα Πόντου·

     νᾶσοί θ᾽ αἱ κατὰ πρῶν᾽ ἅλιον περίκλυστοι
     τᾷδε γᾷ προσήμεναι,
     οἷα Λέσβος ἐλαιόφυτός τε Σάμ-
     ος, Χίος, ἠδὲ Πάρος, Νάξος, Μύκον-
     ος, Τήνῳ τε συνάπτουσ᾽
     Ἄνδρος ἀγχιγείτων.

CHORUS OF PERSIAN ELDERS:

We had an empire once,
                    a paradise of laws and gold.
      A sage was king, an honest man
                  something like a god
                          Darius, monarch of Persia.

Nations bowed down,
                  we lived behind twin shields:
     the army, and the laws on Susa's gate,
                soldiers came home
                      whole in body and mind.

Think of the tribes he ruled
                    without crossing the boundary river
       without leaving the heartland:
              fishermen of Strymon, farmers of Thrace,
                    lake villagers by the gulf.

Men of the hill-forts
              called him lord,
          and the proud Hellespont cities
             guarding Propontis,
                the Black Sea's throat.

Offshore, in sight of our headlands
            Lesbos was ours, olive-laden Samos,
              Chios, Paros, Naxos,
              and Tinos nestled
                  against neighbouring Andros.

Beyond them the deep-sea islands,
                Lemnos and Ikaria, Rhodes and Cnidos
                        Cyprian Paphos and Soli
                                and Salamis, born from the city
                                we shudder to name.

Ionian merchants in their busy towns
                he governed by policy
        not force, our men ambassadors
                                an iron host
                                speaking a hundred tongues.

But the gods are fickle. Suddenly
                we are brought to our knees.
        in a single crushing moment
                                our whole fleet
                        shattered and lost.

Enter XERXES *in his war-chariot, his robes torn.*

XERXES: I never knew a whirlwind could strike
                                from a cloudless sky.
        Some god has made himself our enemy.
                        What is to become of a wretch like me?
        My knees are trembling.
                How can I face these wise old men?
                If I had only met my end with the others.
                        Death would have been an escape.

CHORUS: Ah, king. An army is gone
                and the glory of our empire.
                Our pride
                        our warriors
                                destroyed by an evil demon.

Xerxes has crammed with Persians the halls of hell.
The men of Agdobata, blossoming branches
flower of our land, bowmen, lost, all of them
an incalculable myriad of men.
What was the reward of their courage?
The pride of Asia, king,
lost without trace.

XERXES: And I was born
to bring this calamity on my native land.

CHORUS: Homecoming is an occasion for song.
For you, king
this comfortless ode, black
lament of the Mariandyni, a tune
freighted with tears.

XERXES: Ah, that unending plaintive chant,
evil breath casting my destiny back in my face.

CHORUS: Bowed by grief too heavy to bear
a wave of miseries,
this city mourns.

XERXES: It was the Ionian fleet in battle array
turned the tide of war
gathered up our men
reaping to stubble
the sea's black field,
that ill-omened shore.

CHORUS: Sing out our agony, and let us learn the fate of friends.
Where are the warriors who stood at your shoulder?
Where is Pharandakes?
Sousas?
Pelagon or Agabatas?
Psammis, Dotames,
Sousiskanes
the pride of Agabatana?

XERXES: They were lost
    all in one ship
        a galley from Sidon that ran
           on the rocks of Salamis, dashed
              to splinters on its flinty pebbles.

CHORUS: All lost?
          Where is Pharnuchos?
       The hero Ariomardos?
           Where is lord Seualkes?
       Lilaios,
          oldest and best of councillors?
   Memphis?
 Tharubis?
    Masistros?
       Artembares and Hystaichmas?
         Questions on questions.
            Answer us, king.

XERXES: Just as the ancient walls of Athens
    came into view, at a single stroke
       they gasped out their lives
         in the shallows
           far from their friends.

CHORUS: And the greatest of all the Persians,
       chosen from a thousand thousand,
    the King's Own Eye, Alpistos
       son of Batanochus, where is he?
And Parthos, son of Sesamas, son of Megabates
       and tall Oibares?
     Did you leave them there, did you,
       a cruel word
         to fall on Persian ears?

XERXES: These memories
    are my companions now for ever,
      grief piled on unbearable grief.
My heart is shattered to pieces.

CHORUS: The names come flooding in,
                                the innumerable tribe of Mardoi,
                                Xanthes,
                                        Anachares of the Arians,
                        Diaixis and Arsakes tamers of horses,
                Agdadatas and Lythimnas,
                                Tolmos unwearied in battle,
        all buried under earth, who used to march
                                behind your chariot wheels.

XERXES: Our soldiers, our countrymen, are lost.

CHORUS: All lost, their names erased for ever.

Barbarians Boxing

Every page of the atlas has been half erased
in a swirling cloud of dust, iron filings, blood.
A barbarian boxing, say the Greeks, when you
hit his face, he covers his face, when you hit
his belly, he covers his belly. If both sides
want a fight, does it matter who landed the first
blow, and on what day? In the lit corner
of our ravaged world a tree waits for spring.

Author's Envoy

Well, my page, my familiar, are you so keen
        to offer yourself to every casual browser
In your designer outfit cut from the finest cloth,
        that elegant ornamented jacket?
You've flirted long enough, you imagine, in our
        small set, passed hand to generous hand
Among acquaintances. Your greatest fear? Obscurity,
        alone on the shelf. Poor slave to fame,
This narrative has no second draft. 'What have I
        done?' you'll say, 'What did I imagine?'
That snapper-up of latest fashions will abandon you
        a little dog-eared, with the other castoffs.
So to my friendly prediction: you'll be adored
        till the novelty wears thin, until
Thumbed and a trifle faded you'll find yourself
        set to one side, a moth-eaten outcast
Consigned to a bookstore in the provinces. Since once
        I gave you ample warning, now
I savour my revenge, like the angry muleteer
        who pushed his animal (too stubborn
To be saved) into the ravine. The last indignity?
        Language classes in the outer suburbs.
In gentler times perhaps you'll reach an audience.
        Tell them my ancestors were miners,
Their sons and grandsons fledged and flown
        we inherited everything but wealth.
Say also under dictatorship in Greece I knew
        one of the immortals, and his equal
In bourgeois Britain. Say I was stocky, with
        receding hair, and loved to sit
Under my vine-trellis. Quick to find fault, I was
        easily won over. As for history,
Tell them in the middle of my sixth decade
        Bush and Cheney stole the presidency.

Horace, Epistle 1: 20

PAPER SPECIFICATION / POLEMIC

The Five Seasons 'Original' recycled paper (110 gsm) used for this book is manufactured from one hundred per cent pre-consumer RCF (recovered fibre) sourced from scrap chiefly generated during printing and converting operations in the UK, with some addition of 'mill broke'.

No post-consumer fibre has been specified for this paper. This is because no paper mill in the UK currently manufactures quality recycled publishing papers using UK-sourced post-consumer fibre. Some all- or part-recycled publishing papers made in the UK *do* use MDIP (a market de-inked pulp made from post-consumer paper) but this is *imported*—principally from the USA and to a lesser extent from France. Publishers are being encouraged by various campaigns to specify post-consumer recovered fibre in UK-manufactured book papers but this is *not* reducing the amount of waste printed paper dumped in British landfill sites. The production of these 'environmentally-friendly' papers depends on long-distance pulp shipments.

The Waste & Resources Action Programme (WRAP — www.wrap.org.uk) published a major report in January 2005 on the feasibility of resolving this problem by building a pulp mill in the uk capable of producing the required post-consumer RCF pulp: *Market De-Inked Pulp Facility Pre-Feasibility Study* (ISBN 1-84405-142-0). Its findings suggest that a British MDIP facility is unlikely to be built in the near future because of various economic factors (and no British paper mill 'in the printings and writings sector' has 'shown an immediate interest in direct investment in the proposed MDIP plant').

So for the present Five Seasons Press has decided that the best policy is to promote awareness of this regrettable situation and to continue to use UK pre-consumer rcf rather than us post-consumer RCF in Five Seasons recycled papers. Five Seasons also prefers to specify a one hundred per cent furnish of these locally-recovered fibres rather than combine them with Forest Stewardship Council virgin fibres that, as likely as not, come from Uruguayan eucalyptus pulped in Morocco. Five Seasons Press agrees with WRAP's argument that the promotion of recycled paper *per se* is the critical issue. Improved facilities and options will only become economically viable when the demand for recycled papers (whether pre-consumer or post-consumer) increases.

It is of course much more difficult for a large publishing house than for Five Seasons to specify paper of this quality and (relative) probity. One of the many benefits of small-scale publishing.

Glenn Storhaug, publisher